JB JOSSEY-BASS™
A Wiley Brand

Volunteer Management Essentials for Hospitals & Health-Related Nonprofits

Paul Bartush, Editor

WILEY

Copyright © 2012 by John Wiley & Sons, Inc. All rights reserved.

Originally published by Stevenson, Inc.

Published by John Wiley & Sons, Inc., Hoboken, New Jersey.

No part of this publication may be reproduced, stored in a retrieval system, or transmitted in any form or by any means, electronic, mechanical, photocopying, recording, scanning, or otherwise, except as permitted under Section 107 or 108 of the 1976 United States Copyright Act, without either the prior written permission of the Publisher, or authorization through payment of the appropriate per-copy fee to the Copyright Clearance Center, Inc., 222 Rosewood Drive, Danvers, MA 01923, (978) 750-8400, fax (978) 646-8600, or on the Web at www.copyright.com. Requests to the Publisher for permission should be addressed to the Permissions Department, John Wiley & Sons, Inc., 111 River Street, Hoboken, NJ 07030, (201) 748-6011, fax (201) 748-6008, or online at http://www.wiley.com/go/permissions.

Limit of Liability/Disclaimer of Warranty: While the publisher and author have used their best efforts in preparing this book, they make no representations or warranties with respect to the accuracy or completeness of the contents of this book and specifically disclaim any implied warranties of merchantability or fitness for a particular purpose. No warranty may be created or extended by sales representatives or written sales materials. The advice and strategies contained herein may not be suitable for your situation. You should consult with a professional where appropriate. Neither the publisher nor author shall be liable for any loss of profit or any other commercial damages, including but not limited to special, incidental, consequential, or other damages.

For general information on our other products and services or for technical support, please contact our Customer Care Department within the United States at (800) 762-2974, outside the United States at (317) 572-3993 or fax (317) 572-4002.

Wiley publishes in a variety of print and electronic formats and by print-on-demand. Some material included with standard print versions of this book may not be included in e-books or in print-on-demand. If this book refers to media such as a CD or DVD that is not included in the version you purchased, you may download this material at http://booksupport.wiley.com. For more information about Wiley products, visit www.wiley.com.

978-1-118-69043-7 ISBN

978-1-118-70388-5 ISBN (online)

Volunteer Management Essentials For Hospitals & Health-related Nonprofits

Paul Bartush, Editor

Paul Bartush has been involved in volunteer management for over 15 years. In June of 2009, Paul was appointed as the Director for the Volunteer Department, Medical Interpreter Services, Information Associates and the LVC Retail Shops at MGH.

In his most recent position, he was responsible for the strategic management of a volunteer pool of 900 volunteers, contributing over 100,000 hours of service annually to the hospital in patient experience enhancing roles. In addition, Paul was responsible for the leadership of the Medical Interpreter Services program which delivered services in over 65,000 separate patient encounters in FY2010.

Paul is the immediate past-president of the Massachusetts Association of Directors of Healthcare Volunteer Services and has presented at state, regional and national conferences on the topics of volunteer management, strategic leadership and strategic planning.

Paul has co-authored two publications for the Association for Healthcare Volunteer Resource Professionals. He earned a Masters in Healthcare Management from Cambridge College and a Bachelor of Science in Human Development from The Pennsylvania State University.

He is a member of the Association for Healthcare Volunteer Resource Professionals.

Published by

Stevenson, Inc.

P.O. Box 4528 • Sioux City, Iowa • 51104

Phone 712.239.3010 • Fax 712.239.2166

www.stevensoninc.com

© 2012 by Stevenson, Inc. All rights reserved by the publisher. No part of this publication may be reproduced or transmitted in any form or by any means, electronic or mechanical, including photocopying, recording, or any other information storage or retrieval system, without written permission of the publisher. Violators will be prosecuted. This publication is designed to provide accurate and authoritative information in regard to the subject matter covered. It is sold with the understanding that the publisher is not engaged in legal, accounting or other professional services. If legal or other expert assistance is required, the services of a competent professional person should be sought. (From a Declaration of Principles jointly adopted by a committee of the American Bar Association and a committee of publishers.) Stevenson, Inc., does not necessarily endorse any products or services mentioned.

Table of Contents

© 2012 Stevenson, Inc. Published 2012 by Stevenson, Inc.

There are some basic practices that should be in place for any volunteer management program to achieve the fullest degree of success. For starters, it's well worth your time to put together a yearlong (or multiyear) plan for your department. Your final document should include: goals, quantifiable objectives required to achieve those goals, action plans that spell out how you intend to achieve each objective and a master calendar that outlines the details of what needs to happen throughout the year.

Have a Written Plan in Place for Your Volunteer Program

Does your volunteer department have a written plan in place that outlines its goals for the next one, three or even five years?

If not, set aside time to create one. Having a written plan in place is an effective way to not only spell out what is expected to occur over that time frame, but what is necessary to achieve each of the goals.

Every year as the fiscal year winds down for Home & Hospice Care of Rhode Island (Pawtucket, RI), Bobbi Wexler, volunteer program manager, spends a few hours weekly over the next four months developing a comprehensive written plan outlining her department's goals and objectives.

Her department's goals are tied to the four primary areas of the organization's overall strategic plan — patient services, community outreach, staff development and caregiver support.

Some of the goals for the nonprofit that are identified annually include:

- ✓ targeted number of volunteers to be trained as patient volunteers, administrative volunteers and complementary therapists;
- ✓ volunteer utilization rates (inpatient unit, home teams and long-term care facilities); and
- ✓ program activities and implementation with dates identified for planning, startup and responsible party.

> Be prepared to explain the on boarding process the time involved from start to finish and what individuals can do to expedite the process when and if possible. Having a clear process outlined shows that you are organized and available to assist in the process of becoming a volunteer.

Wexler shares the plan's development process, step by step:

1. During September she asks the senior leadership team (e.g., president/CEO, vice presidents and directors) for their comments/concerns and goals/plans they have regarding the volunteer program.
2. Each October, Wexler meets for an afternoon retreat with staff of four volunteer coordinators. The retreat has three objectives: team building; evaluating prior year's accomplishments/challenges; and identifying a program plan for the upcoming year.
3. Following the retreat, Wexler integrates ideas she has gathered from the senior leadership team and her staff and develops a program plan for the next 12 to 15 months. This plan, which includes goals, measurable objectives, target dates and responsible parties, is then presented to the senior leadership team for approval.

The result of this extensive effort is an invaluable tool used year-round throughout the nonprofit: A four-page plan, distributed to key staff, is updated as needed, looked at monthly by Wexler and reviewed quarterly by senior leadership.

To help other volunteer managers get started crafting their own written plan, Wexler shares her sample program plan for 2008, below.

Source: Bobbi Wexler, Volunteer Program Manager, Home & Hospice Care of Rhode Island, Pawtucket, RI.
E-mail: bwexler@hhcri.org

Content not available in this edition

Confirm Volunteer Assignments in Writing

What tools do you provide your volunteers to help them succeed?

As you work with multiple numbers of volunteers on projects requiring individualized follow-up, your odds of having them complete assigned tasks will improve significantly if you provide each volunteer with written confirmation of what to do, and by when.

Whenever you conduct a meeting in which volunteers leave with agreed-to tasks, immediately send them a personalized memo — as opposed to a standardized group memo — confirming their duties. Spell out exactly what is expected of them, and be sure to include a deadline for the project (or multiple deadlines for portions of the project).

In addition to delineating each task, clearly state how to report back or turn in completed work. This helps bring closure to the task.

Here are two techniques you may want to include in your memo:

1. Offer an incentive for completing tasks on time.
2. Add a final sentence to your memo indicating that all persons not having completed their tasks by the stated deadline will be contacted by you (or the appropriate person) to determine what needs to happen in order to finish the project. Adding a closing statement such as this motivates volunteers to avoid the embarrassment of being contacted and provides you with a justifiable reason for following up with them.

Electronic Timesheet Streamlines Volunteer Tracking

Managing nearly 450 volunteers can be a challenge, but officials at Hospice Austin (www.hospiceaustin.org) of Austin, TX, have found an electronic timesheet to be of great assistance in tracking volunteer hours.

Volunteers at Hospice Austin complete an electronic timesheet — available on the nonprofit's website at www.hospiceaustin.org/site/pp.asp?c=bdJPITMyA&b=14556 — each time they work in the office; facilitate a support group; provide community education; help with an event; or have patient contact, either by phone or in person.

McCranie outlines a process that illustrates the importance of what she is asking of her volunteers by telling them what she does with the notes that they send with their timesheets.

When volunteers completes their online timesheets and submit them, Hospice officials automatically receive a copy. Volunteer coordinators can then read notes on the timesheets to see if any particular information needs to be shared with other members of the interdisciplinary team. A copy of each timesheet is printed and sent to the medical records department to be scanned into that patient's chart.

Tracking volunteer hours carefully helps staff determine the cost savings provided by volunteers. It helps meet statutes requiring hospice organizations that receive Medicare reimbursements to provide at least five percent of all direct patient care through volunteers. And tracking all volunteer time — not just what is directly related to patient or family care — also provides information needed to apply for grants.

"In order to encourage volunteers to complete their timesheets, we help them understand that by doing so they are assisting us in meeting the Medicare regulation, as well as helping us fulfill our mission to provide the highest quality, patient-centered care possible," says Nancy Chester McCranie, director of volunteer and bereavement services.

"Along with their time, there is a place on the timesheet for volunteers to provide information about what happened during their visit. That information can then be shared with other members of the interdisciplinary team," she says. "This kind of communication is invaluable in the work we do. So, our volunteers understand that it's not just a timesheet, it's a way of staying connected and being a part of the bigger picture and a part of the mission of our agency."

Source: Nancy Chester McCranie, Director of Volunteer and Bereavement Services, Hospice Austin, Austin, TX. E-mail: nmccranie@hospiceaustin.org

Tips for Promoting Volunteer Timesheet Completion

Even the most carefully planned systems will struggle without buy-in from users. Here Nancy Chester McCranie, director of volunteer and bereavement services, Hospice Austin (Austin, TX), offers the following tips to promote volunteer timesheet completion:

- Make it as simple and straightforward as possible for everyone concerned.
- Help volunteers understand how tracking hours helps the organization fulfill its mission.
- Give frequent reminders to turn in time sheets that note why it is important to the organization's work and constituents.
- Give frequent praise for turning in hours.
- Share with volunteers the end result, so they can see how their efforts made a difference.

How Do You Supervise Your Volunteers?

Supervisors' styles vary from nonprofit to nonprofit based upon the organization's size, needs, mission, goals and other factors. Here, two people who work with volunteers share their techniques and tips:

- **Heather Powers, volunteer coordinator, Condell Medical Center Hospice (Libertyville, IL),** has nine teen and 16 adult volunteers. She takes a direct role in supervision, going to see volunteers in action once a quarter, including accompanying them on home visits. She also holds roundtable discussion meetings with volunteers every other month, which not only allows volunteers to talk out issues, but also lets Powers gauge how they are doing with a patient or patient-related issues.
- **Shawnee Parsil, director of volunteer services, HospiceCare Inc. (Madison, WI),** says with 950 volunteers, she relies on staff to help directly supervise them. She takes an active role to make sure staff give volunteers feedback and support. In fact, the hospice's mission and vision statement includes "appreciating the time and energy gifted by volunteers." She constantly reminds staff, "Everyone who works with a volunteer is a volunteer manager." She and the volunteer coordinators get feedback from staff. If a situation does arise with a volunteer, staff and the volunteer services department team up to resolve the problem.

Source: Shawnee Parsil, Director of Volunteer Services, HospiceCare Inc., Madison, WI.
E-mail: sparsil@hospicecareinc.com
Heather Powers, Volunteer Coordinator, Condell Medical Center Hospice, Libertyville, IL. E-mail: hpowers@condell.org

Advisory Council Directs, Advocates for Volunteer Program

Creating a volunteer advisory council at your nonprofit can offer your volunteer department the advocacy and direction needed to maintain a strong volunteer force. At the Seattle Cancer Care Alliance (Seattle, WA), dedicated supporters serve two-year terms on an 18-member volunteer advisory council tasked with helping shape the scope of the volunteer services division.

Members of the volunteer advisory council, which is approaching its 20th anniversary, are elected annually. Leadership positions include a president; vice president, who also chairs the development committee; event chairperson; and newsletter chairperson.

"The key to our council is that it is an active and working council," says Erica Karlovits, volunteer services manager. "It's imperative to get people who will be active and can dedicate the time to the council."

Among the council's duties are assisting with volunteer communication and education, as well as developing effective in-services and orientations. It facilitates volunteer preparation for accreditation surveys by conducting monthly mock surveys to offer feedback to staff and ensure information in orientation is being absorbed. It also administers volunteer satisfaction surveys every two years.

The events committee, a segment of the advisory council, provides social events for patients and families. It also orients and recruits new members to the council, and works to educate and develop new leaders throughout the program.

"We try to have our council be as representative of our overall volunteer population as possible, so we attempt to incorporate age diversity as well as gender, cultural and role diversity throughout the council," says Karlovits.

Volunteers serving on the council must have volunteered for a minimum of one year. However, if a new program area is developed, exceptions are made to bring on representatives from new program areas, allowing each segment of volunteer services to have a voice on the advisory council.

"Members of the council are the champions of our programs. We make sure they know the leadership of our program well, which helps us to gain support for the volunteer program," says Karlovits.

"The council is apprised of financial reporting, so they're fully aware of impacts to the department, and we rely on them to advise us on all facets of volunteer services. They are huge stakeholders in our volunteer department."

Source: Erica Karlovits, Manager of Volunteer Services, Seattle Cancer Care Alliance, Seattle, WA.
E-mail: ekarlovi@seattlecca.org

Bylaws Help Govern Council

If your organization is considering adding a leadership council to your volunteer organization, create bylaws that will help govern this representative model of volunteer leadership.

When developing the bylaws for your newly formed volunteer advisory council, take a lesson from the Seattle Cancer Care Alliance (Seattle, WA), and add some or all of the following sections to your bylaws:

- Purpose of the council
- Definitions and working terms
- Scope of authority
- Meetings details
- Officers
- Membership
- Resignation and removal procedures

Distinguish Between Employee and Volunteer

Many employees of nonprofits also volunteer with the organization. To help manage this important subgroup of volunteers, consider establishing a policy that lets staff know what the employee volunteer can or can't do.

Marti Coplai, life enrichment/volunteer coordinator, The Residence of Arbor Hospice (Ann Arbor, MI), says she has a couple staff members who volunteer as "By Your Side" companions. These volunteers offer companionship and support to hospice patients during the night hours.

Coplai knows the importance of emphasizing the distinction between on-the-clock employees and employees on volunteer duty. She has a list of expectations outlined in the position training manual for the volunteer and staff.

One important point? The nursing staff should not expect the employee/volunteer to perform his/her regular job duties when the person is volunteering as a companion.

Beyond protecting the employee's rights as set out in the Fair Labor Standards Act (employers cannot ask staff to perform a duty, similar to their regular job description, without compensation), Coplai says the list of expectations protects the volunteer and the organization.

She says she wants staff to respect the boundaries of the volunteer and treat them as volunteers, not staff, when they are performing the companion role.

To help staff members clearly define when they are volunteering, she provides them with volunteer nametags and stresses that when they are wearing the nametag, they are volunteers, not paid staff.

During the training for the companion program, Coplai not only goes over the expectations in the manual, but also will explain to the employee volunteers what lines should not be crossed. For example, if an information technology employee wants to volunteer, staff should not be asking that person to work on their computer problems while the technologist is volunteering as a companion.

Source: Marti Coplai, Life Enrichment/Volunteer Coordinator, The Residence of Arbor Hospice, Ann Arbor, MI. E-mail: mcoplai@arborhospice.org

Provide Guidelines for Your Employee Volunteers

When employees wish to volunteer within your organization, should they have to follow specific guidelines to do so? Absolutely, says Alfreda Rooks, director of volunteer services at the University of Michigan Health System (UMHS), Ann Arbor, MI. "Having guidelines insures that the employee is aware that there are boundaries between being an employee and being a volunteer.

"We have a clearly defined code of conduct and behavior expectations for all volunteers, including those volunteers who are employed by UMHS," says Rooks. "The guidelines help to avoid any possible conflicts that may arise, before they happen."

Every volunteer must complete a volunteer application, provide two written references and undergo a background check.

"Because criminal history background checks currently only occur when you are a new hire, the director of security recommends that employees who volunteer be screened the same as current volunteers," says Rooks. Since employees undergo a yearly health screening, they do not need to do the new volunteer health screening.

Typically, employees wishing to volunteer at the hospital come from clerical or other support positions, Rooks says. And while many employees choose to volunteer in an effort to change their career or get experience, Rooks says there are issues to consider when having employees volunteer. "Employees wishing to volunteer in traditional volunteer roles, for example, on patient floors are discouraged from volunteering in the same role for which they are paid. We would discourage a nurse from volunteering in a clinical/nursing support role."

> *"Guidelines serve as a reminder to the employee that during the time they volunteer, their behavior cannot be that of an employee ... This protects the patients they come in contact with and the employee in their volunteer role."*

On average, the medical facility has more than 1,600 volunteers on hand. For persons currently employed with the health system, there is a special link on the UMHS Volunteer Services website (www.med.umich.edu/volunteer) stating the guidelines.

Says Rooks, "Guidelines serve as a reminder to the employee that during the time they volunteer, their behavior cannot be that of an employee, for example, offering suggestions, services, etc. Nor can they function in their employee role. This protects the patients they come in contact with and the employee in their volunteer role."

Source: Alfreda R. Rooks, Director of Volunteer Services, University of Michigan Health System. Ann Arbor, MI. E-mail: arooks@umich.edu

Build Skills, Advance Career With Professional Certification

Becoming Certified in Volunteer Administration (CVA) can offer volunteer managers a boost in credibility, confidence, and professionalism.

The Council for Certification in Volunteer Administration (CCVA) in Midlothian, VA, offers an international certification program that is performance based. This self-study program measures an individual's application of knowledge and skills for those with at least 3 years of real-life experience in this role. "We have candidates from all types of settings, and in all kinds of positions related to volunteer engagement," says Katherine Campbell, executive director of CCVA. "We have anecdotal evidence that a professional credential such as the CVA can help people keep their jobs, have their roles upgraded or better positioned within the organization, and be more competitive when searching for jobs."

The CCVA program evaluates candidates' competencies based on ethics, organizational management, human resource management, accountability and leadership and advocacy.

There are two parts of the CVA certification process:

Part I: Portfolio

- **Philosophy Statement** — personal reflection on beliefs and values related to one's role as a leader and manager of volunteers.
- **Ethics Case Study** — description of a work-related situation involving ethics and how it relates to the profession's core values.
- **Management Narrative** — description and analysis of a project or activities focused on core competencies.

Part II: Multiple Choice Examination

The CVA test is made up of 80 multiple choice questions. It is a two-hour proctored examination, taken online.

For more information on CVA go to www.cvacert.org.

Source: Katherine H. Campbell, Executive Director, Council for Certification in Volunteer Administration, Midlothian, VA. E-mail: ccva@comcast.net

Market Your Volunteer Program Internally

As one of hundreds of nurses at the Mayo Health System, Joyce White had no idea of the number of volunteers required to keep the hospital running. When White became director of volunteer services at the Mayo Clinic in Florida (Jacksonville, FL), she says she was surprised to learn the number was so large — currently 800 and growing.

"I felt as though this vital part of our workforce was 'lost' in the midst of us, and that is unfair to both employees and volunteers," says White. "I've found that employees have a greater respect for volunteers, once they clearly understand their potential and limitations."

Today, White uses many approaches to sell management and other employees on the clinic's volunteer efforts. One way is through a summer teen program.

"All managers are e-mailed to see if they are interested in hosting a teen in their department for the summer," she explains. Through this process, she says, not only does the clinic receive additional volunteers, the managers who oversee them come to understand more about volunteering, as do employees whose teen children volunteer.

As another effort to connect staff with volunteers and the impact they make, White posts pictures of all volunteers, sorted by department, on the hospital's intranet system.

When approached with a request for a new volunteer service, White says she looks at the big picture. "Often I can conceptualize a model that is more efficient or more meaningful to the volunteers. It is a collaborative effort to meet both Mayo's and the volunteers' needs," she says. Once a new service area is established, she educates team leaders and/or staff on how to manage the volunteers.

In addition to being aware of volunteers, White says management must be aware of volunteers' contributions, especially when trying to fill paid positions. "Management should know the value of volunteer contributions when they consider budgetary changes. Further, managers have more of a tendency to include volunteers when discussing issues with employees. After all, both are part of our workforce; one is just unpaid."

Holding staff accountable for recruiting and retaining volunteers keeps everyone involved and aware of volunteer opportunities. At the Florida clinic, White says physicians often refer patients while some staff spread the word to friends and family.

But what if your organization works on a much smaller scale?

The Big Brothers Big Sisters of Metro Milwaukee (Milwaukee, WI) has just 25 employees, but supports about 1,500 volunteer mentoring relationships annually, says Jan Nowak, vice president of marketing.

And while it may be tempting to assume that at a smaller nonprofit everyone knows what's going on, it's just as important as it is at a large nonprofit to keep internal communication lines open, Nowak says. She says monthly senior staff meetings are a great way to keep everyone in the loop and generate even stronger and more successful ideas.

"Since we are a smaller organization, our personal relationships are closer," she says. "This helps to create a different type of enthusiasm when discussing new ideas."

Sources: Jan Nowak, Big Brothers Big Sisters of Metro Milwaukee, Milwaukee, WI. E-mail: bfehlauer@bbbsmilwaukee.org
Joyce White, Director of Volunteer Services, Mayo Clinic Florida, Jacksonville, FL. E-mail: white.joyce@mayo.edu

Fit Volunteer Positions Into Busy Lives

"I don't have the time."

How often do you hear that phrase when trying to recruit volunteers?

Today more than ever, traditional volunteer roles, with set times and days, don't necessarily appeal to volunteers with young children and careers or retirees who enjoy the freedom of their lifestyle. Keeping your volunteer base strong and satisfied means adjusting to volunteers' lifestyles, says Christina Johnson, volunteer coordinator, Ronald McDonald House (Louisville, KY).

Johnson says she saw how difficult the "I don't have the time" phrase made it to recruit volunteers for regular shift positions. So she created multiple positions that were flexible and open to families and groups, then advertised them in her new brochure.

The four-page, 8 X 10-inch color brochure (shown, at right) details five different volunteer positions that can be done from home or as a onetime event, and which fit into whatever time the volunteer has available.

The five positions are:

- **Adopt-A-Meal** gives groups of no more than eight the opportunity to fix a home-cooked meal for 50 residents, or drop off a casserole to use in a pinch.
- **Wish List Drive** volunteers drop off needed food, cleaning and toiletry items.
- **Host an Event** volunteers plan a fun night of entertainment for houseguests.
- **Volunteer from Home** volunteers and families put together goodie bags for families, make cards of encouragement and snacks and save drink can pull-tabs for the house.
- **Community Service** volunteers come in groups to clean, bake snacks or decorate.

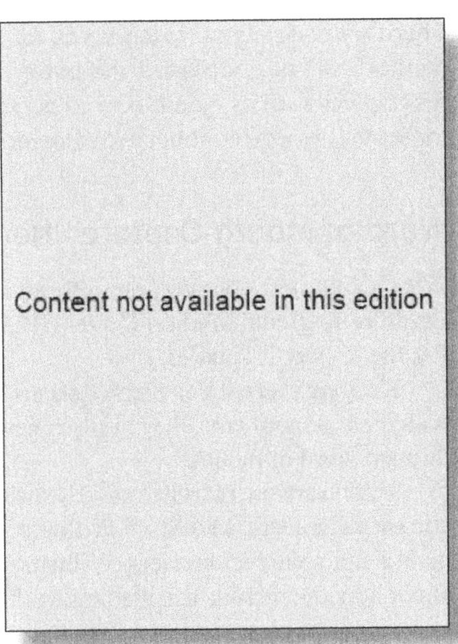

Johnson says each position is flexible and works with the volunteer's schedule. Since positions are always supervised, volunteers can start right away, without going through an application and screening process. Plus, while Johnson offers guidelines and ideas for the volunteers, she also welcomes and supports their suggestions, saying some of the best ideas have come from volunteers.

When the new volunteer positions were created, Johnson says she could spend 20 minutes explaining them to folks on the phone. That's one reason she created the brochure shown here. Now, Johnson gets callers' contact information and sends them a brochure they can look at and share with their group.

She also hands out the colorful, easy-to-read brochures at volunteer fairs, stuffed with a wish list.

Source: Christina Johnson, Volunteer Coordinator, Ronald McDonald House Louisville, Louisville, KY.
E-mail: Christina@rmhlouisville.org

© 2012 Stevenson, Inc. Published 2012 by Stevenson, Inc.

General and Targeted Recruitment Ideas

There are a variety of methods you can use to recruit volunteers, some of which are shared here. General recruitment methods will be your bread-and-butter tools, but there will be times when recruitment will be targeted at particular demographics such as youth, retired persons and corporate volunteers. Keep testing new ways of reaching out, and don't forget that word-of-mouth recruitment from active volunteers may be your most successful recruitment method.

Word of Mouth Captures New Volunteers

What's your best volunteer recruitment method? For the Bradford Regional Medical Center (BRMC) of Bradford, PA, the answer is simple:

Keeping current volunteers so satisfied and pleased with their assignments, they bring in new volunteers through word of mouth.

Volunteers are recruited strictly through referral from current volunteers, says Stacy Williams, director of annual giving and volunteer services. Williams answers questions about how the recruitment method works:

How many volunteers do you work with at BRMC?

"We average 250 volunteers per month with average hours served last year (2008) of 2,214 per month."

How many volunteers do you obtain from word-of-mouth recruitment?

"All are word of mouth. We do not do any type of recruiting with the exception of our hospice volunteers."

Do you encourage the word-of-mouth recruitment or do the volunteers just go ahead and do it based on their positive experiences?

"The volunteers recruit on their own. The volunteers enjoy their work experience and are eager to share their experience with family and friends. We also have volunteers who staff our information desk, so when individuals present at the desk inquiring about volunteering, the volunteer on staff will share the process of becoming a volunteer and their personal experience."

What is it about BRMC that makes volunteers want to recruit others?

"The volunteers feel a sense of pride and gratification in the work they do. They want to share that experience with others and allow others the opportunity to make a difference."

How is the board of directors made aware of volunteer efforts?

"As the director of volunteers, each month I provide the board of directors a report that reveals how many hours are donated to the hospital and to what areas. Our board and senior management are very appreciative and impressed by the dedication of our volunteers."

How is this appreciation reflected back to the volunteers? What rewards do they receive?

"To the volunteers, I believe, it is the lasting friendships formed with employees at the medical center. Some of the perks they receive are discounts in the cafeteria and gift shop. Volunteer staff also receive free coffee, tea, soda and more. They're included in the annual holiday party, summer picnic and wellness events. Each spring, volunteers are also invited to an appreciation luncheon in their honor, and we celebrate anniversary dates of their years of service. We have 12 volunteers with more than 20 years of service and two volunteers with more than 40 years of service. That's dedication!"

Source: Stacy Williams, Director of Annual Giving and Volunteer Services, Bradford Regional Medical Center, Bradford, PA. E-mail: swilliams@brmc.com

Target Boomers With Posters

Volunteers from the baby boomer generation (born 1946 to 1964) tend to be long-term volunteers steadfast in their devotion to volunteer efforts. That's one reason why Diane Rhodes, volunteer services manager, Sutter Medical Center Sacramento (Sacramento, CA), specifically targets recruitment efforts at persons age 55 and over.

Volunteers at the medical center and cancer center already total 450, but Rhodes says she hopes to attract 50 to 100 more volunteers in the boomer category.

One way she is doing so is through an eye-catching poster designed to capture the spirit of the organization and draw the attention of mature volunteers. Placed strategically throughout the cancer center and hospitals, the poster features a picture of a youthful senior, the words, "Give Something Back!" and contact information.

Rhodes shares tips to create an effective recruitment poster:

- Create a clean, simple poster that prominently displays contact information.
- Use appropriate visuals, such as a photo of someone volunteering.
- Use vibrant, engaging text on your poster that will speak directly to your target audience.

Source: Diane Rhodes, Volunteer Services Manager, Sutter Medical Center Sacramento, Sacramento, CA. E-mail: RhodesD2@sutterhealth.org

Guide Current Volunteers to Help Recruit New Volunteers

The opening of the newest hospital for St. John Health (Detroit, MI) required a massive volunteer recruitment campaign. The goal: Fill 730 four-hour shifts for the new Providence Park Hospital (Novi, MI). Hospital officials reached that goal, thanks to a multifaceted recruitment campaign and the help of current volunteers.

Kathy Zaguroli, manager of volunteer services/ CareLink at Providence Park Hospital and Providence Hospital (Southfield, MI), says current volunteers played a crucial role in filling those positions.

"Existing volunteers are your best recruitment tool and usually have a broad network of contacts in the community," she says.

As the only staff member in the volunteer office at the new location, Zaguroli depended heavily on volunteers. The recruitment committee asked all volunteers to share fliers and press releases with family and friends. Veteran volunteers greeted attendees and conducted mini-interviews at a three-hour volunteer recruitment fair; and Zaguroli trained teams to conduct formal interviews and weekly orientation sessions.

When seeking a large number of new volunteers, Zaguroli offers additional advice: "Plan, plan, plan, and don't compromise quality for quantity. You still need to do due diligence with screening to meet your needs, not just to have warm bodies."

Source: Kathy Zaguroli, Manager of Volunteer Services/ CareLink, Providence Park Hospital and Providence Hospital, Novi, MI. E-mail: kathleen.zaguroli@stjohn.org

Get More Responses From Recruitment Brochures

To get more responses from your recruitment brochures, make it easy for volunteers to respond to them.

When Jane Karaman, manager, volunteer services, Northeast Hospitals (Beverly, MA), saw a brochure with a tear-off, self-addressed, stamped postcard that persons could easily use if interested in volunteering, she knew she wanted a similar design for her recruitment brochure.

Karaman asked her marketing department to design a new brochure with a similar self-addressed, stamped postcard attached to it.

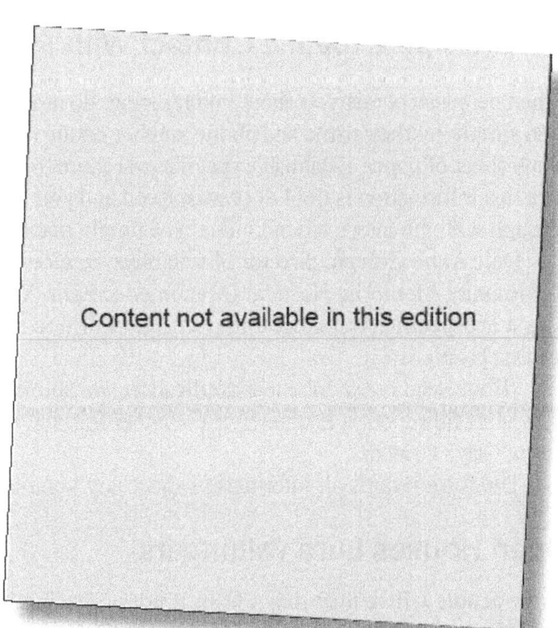

The new, sleekly designed brochures (shown at right) may be an extra expense, but they're worth it, Karaman says. Not only are they a public face for the volunteer department and the hospital, but also since they were added to the hospitals' recruitment repertoire, responses have noticeably increased.

"It's painless to tear off the card and put it in the mailbox," she says.

When volunteers do contact her from the brochure, she mails them her old brochure, which gives detailed descriptions of all her volunteer opportunities. She says both brochures work together but each has a different purpose. The old brochure, created in Microsoft Word, could be printed from Karaman's computer, but was not as eye-catching or as easy to respond to as the new design, she says.

Source: Jane Karaman, Manager of Volunteer Services, Northeast Hospitals, Beverly, MA. E-mail: jkaraman@nhs-healthlink.org

Contact Lapsed Volunteers for Quick Recruitment

When you need to fill volunteer positions quickly, consider contacting your inactive volunteers. They've been trained, they know your organization, and visiting with them may help you learn why they left and fix any problems.

Christie Truly, volunteer coordinator, Appalachian Community Hospice (Athens, OH), says when she came on as volunteer coordinator, she realized the need for more volunteers in areas involving direct patient contact. To get people in fast, she grabbed a list of lapsed volunteers and the phone.

> Illustrating the ease of coming back into the program after a lapse of time takes the burden off of the volunteer who may feel as though he/she needs to explain their departure.

"I introduced myself and got them talking about hospice and why they haven't volunteered for a while," Truly recalls. "I also asked them if they would consider coming back."

Two volunteers came back right away and two more within the month. They received brief refreshers, but many remembered their training on the subjects of grief and death and dying, and were able to step right back in to volunteering.

Interestingly, Truly notes, some of the reasons these persons had quit volunteering resolved on their own and the people just needed someone to reconnect them to the organization. For example, one volunteer had moved, but had since returned to the community and had the same phone number. Another person had been dealing with personal issues that resolved before Truly called.

Phoning lapsed volunteers, Truly was able to learn and address why they had left. Some said they left because they felt there wasn't much for them to do. Truly immediately told them how they were needed and why.

Other volunteers said they dropped out because of lack of time and not being able to fit volunteer hours into the previous schedule. Truly introduced them to her newly created program that gives fully trained hospice volunteers the opportunity to be on-call and come in on nights and weekends.

Source: Christie Truly, Volunteer Coordinator, Appalachian Community Hospice, Athens, OH. E-mail: ctruly@acvna.org

Form Helps Expedite Contact With Prospective Volunteers

When persons contact you about volunteering, do more than simply jot their name and phone number on the nearest blank sheet of paper. Establish a specific procedure to make sure this information is not lost or misplaced and you follow through with the interested individual in a timely manner.

Dale Anne Craven, director of volunteer services, Community Memorial Hospital (Menomonee Falls, WI), uses a Prospective Volunteer Initial Contact Form to alleviate this problem.

"If we send out a volunteer application, we automatically start filling out a Prospective Volunteer Initial Contact Form," says Craven.

The form retains all information about any volunteer who shows interest in the organization and allows staff to enter this information into a database. Two copies of the form are made — one for Craven to make notations on and one for the front office file. Craven tracks dates such as orientation timelines and notes areas of interest of each volunteer to help determine placement.

This form also records when a volunteer application is sent and received, when an interview is scheduled and where the person is assigned.

Source: Dale Anne Craven, Director of Volunteer Services, Community Memorial Hospital, Menomonee Falls, WI. E-mail: dcraven@communitymemorial.com

Open Houses Lure Volunteers

Show people where they might fit in at your organization through an open house.

Patricia Fenner, president, Northumberland Hills Hospital Auxiliary (Cobourg, Ontario, Canada), credits open houses with helping attract more than 110 new volunteers over three years.

"The open house allows our already-working volunteers to communicate in a personal way with potential members, giving them a broad, living idea of what we are about," says Fenner.

Open houses held in the hospital's education centre spotlight three areas supported by volunteers:

- ✓ Ambulatory Care — Pictures and items are displayed representing the area. Handouts outline tasks.
- ✓ Inpatient/Program Support Services — This area, similar to the ambulatory care area, offers information representing its specific services.
- ✓ Fundraising — Materials outline ongoing fundraisers and special events. The hospital's two retail shops also set up displays.

Volunteers staff a sign-up area with volunteer applications and brochures, and take attendees on facility tours, while a Microsoft PowerPoint presentation runs continuously throughout the event.

Source: Patricia Fenner, President, Northumberland Hills Hospital Auxiliary, Cobourg, Ontario, Canada. E-mail: pfenner@nhh.ca

Recruit Volunteers With the Help of the Media

If your organization is in need of volunteers, consider asking the media to help you recruit.

Staff with Casa Grande Regional Medical Center (CGRMC) of Casa Grande, AZ, rely heavily on persons involved in its Summer Student Volunteer Program. But, each year as summer comes to a close and students head back to school, Karen Kerr-Osman, volunteer coordinator, finds herself in need of volunteers.

So she turned to the news media for help.

When a local newspaper reporter was interviewing her about the student volunteer program, Kerr-Osman mentioned her need for volunteers when the student program ends.

A month later, CGRMC's volunteer program was once again in the news, this time as a front-page article with four color photos.

While the focus of this story was on retired adult volunteers, the article also detailed the hospital's volunteer program and its ongoing need for volunteers. It even mentioned the shifts and departments with open positions.

"Publicity is always wonderful," Kerr-Osman says. "You never know who will read it, and if it will be the exact opportunity that they have been seeking. It is an excellent way to reach out to a wider audience."

Although it is too early to tell how many people will inquire about volunteering because of this article, Kerr-Osman says she knows the media works. Several years ago she wrote an article that appeared in a local magazine. She received calls for six months after its publication.

Source: Karen Kerr-Osman, Volunteer Coordinator, Casa Grande Regional Medical Center, Casa Grande, AZ. E-mail: kkerr-osman@cgrmc.org

Tips for Working With the Media

Karen Kerr-Osman, volunteer coordinator, Casa Grande Regional Medical Center (Casa Grande, AZ), recommends the following tips when working with the media to recruit volunteers:

- ✓ **Cultivate a relationship.** Develop a rapport with a reporter, preferably one who regularly covers your organization or writes human-interest articles.
- ✓ **Pitch a story idea.** "Take the time to do it," Kerr-Osman says. "As busy as we all are, the media can do a lot to help us recruit."
- ✓ **Include numbers.** When pitching an idea, remember that numbers speak. Let them know the number of volunteers your facility has, the hours they contribute and number of people served to illustrate the value of the program.
- ✓ **Prepare.** Know the story you want to tell.
- ✓ **Include volunteers.** Giving the volunteers a chance to speak for themselves and tell their story is valuable, she says. It is also important to give the volunteers time to prepare. "I made sure the volunteers were aware ahead of time that the reporter was coming and might interview and photograph them," she says. "This gave them time to think through what they might want to say about the hospital, volunteering and their specific area of service."
- ✓ **Say thanks.** Let the media know you appreciate their support and assistance in promoting your program.

Ask Corporations to Recruit Holiday Volunteers

Many organizations rely heavily on volunteers to bring holiday events to life. But when an event requires more volunteers than you have, where can you turn for help?

One source is large area employers such as businesses and corporations, says Kitty Correll, volunteer chairperson, Children's Healthcare of Atlanta's 2008 holiday events.

"In today's economy, companies are a lot more willing to help find volunteers rather than donate financially," says Correll. "The key is getting to the right person in the corporation."

Once you have contacted the appropriate individual, Correll says, explain the fiscal need and forge an emotional connection or appeal.

To fill some 600 volunteer positions needed for this year's holiday events benefiting Children's Healthcare of Atlanta, Correll says she is relying on area businesses, turning to tried-and-true sources such as local sororities, fraternities and high schools, as well as welcoming community members who come forth thanks to word-of-mouth advertising.

Source: Kitty Correll, 2008 Holiday Chairperson, Children's Healthcare of Atlanta, Atlanta, GA

© 2012 Stevenson, Inc. Published 2012 by Stevenson, Inc.

The thoroughness with which you screen and assess prospective volunteers will impact your program's success in a variety of ways, including volunteer satisfaction levels, volunteers' ability to get the job done right and many more. Taking time to interview would-be volunteers, asking them the right questions and determining the best placement of those who make the grade are, therefore, of vital importance.

Conduct the Right Check for the Right Position

Volunteer screening policies are essential aspects of organizational risk management, says Linda Graff, president of Linda Graff and Associates Inc. (Dundas, Ontario, Canada) and author of "Beyond Police Checks: The Definitive Volunteer and Employee Screening Guidebook." Here, Graff shares advice on building a screening program suited to your organization's volunteer opportunities.

What do nonprofits need to better understand about volunteer screening?

"That one size does not fit all. Screening should be determined by the demands, nature and responsibilities of any given position. An organization needs only basic contact information about a volunteer distributing Gatorade at a marathon, whereas a volunteer providing medical or financial services would need a much more thorough screening."

Do any screening trends span the great diversity of volunteer positions?

"In general, I would say there is too much emphasis on police and criminal checks, and not enough emphasis on identity verification and qualification checks — making sure people know how to write the code they say they do, know how to properly operate the equipment they say they do."

Do you feel any procedures are consistently underutilized?

"Nonprofits seriously underestimate the value of reference checks, in my opinion. The ultimate goal of screening is predicting future behavior, and one of the best indicators of that is past behavior. Reference checks ... when done well, can be very helpful."

When is in-house screening appropriate and when should third-party checking services be considered?

"Outside companies are not necessarily better or more thorough, but they can be contracted to go deeper and get more comprehensive information than an organization can do itself. I think the reason more organizations are turning to them is a recognition that appropriate screening takes time and involves hard costs. The decision of when to move out-of-house really depends on the capacity and skill of in-house screening personnel, the volume of volunteers you have and the drain of screening on staff time and resources."

Criminal and police checks often dominate discussions of volunteer screening. What role do/should these play?

"Because criminal checks are cumbersome and often relatively ineffective, they should be reserved for positions of trust involving one or more of the following situations: access to vulnerable populations, access to money or other valuables and access to confidential, private, personal or otherwise privileged information. But it's important to keep in mind that criminal record checks are not foolproof."

Many organizations worry that the hassle or intrusion of screening will turn off potential volunteers. What do you say to such concerns?

"This is a long-past myth that has simply been discredited. Most potential volunteers now recognize that if you are going to put people in a position of trust, you have a responsibility to ensure that they are trustworthy. The word is pretty much out on the street on that, and not too many people will be surprised or put off by screening anymore.

"More than that, though, people's response to screening depends on the way it is introduced and explained. If you have a disgruntled screener who feels like he is doing busy work, potential volunteers will naturally feel that their time is being wasted. If people understand the purpose of policies and why they are necessary, though, they will be much more patient with the process. When screening is explained well, the loss rate is very, very low."

Do you have any cautions for individuals overseeing volunteer screening?

"People need to understand that volunteer screening is just the first phase of risk management. Once you have people placed, you need to do everything you can — checking on them, connecting with them, supervising them, calling them to account when they are not meeting standards — to make sure you continue to have the right person in the right job."

Source: Linda Graff, President, Linda Graff and Associates Inc., Dundas, Ontario, Canada. E-mail: LL.GRAFF@sympatico.ca

Tools Help You Assess Your Volunteer Corps

When it comes to background checks, is your volunteer screening program stuck in the police-check-or-nothing frame of mind? Linda Graff, president of Linda Graff and Associates Inc. (Dundas, Ontario, Canada) and author of "Beyond Police Checks: The Definitive Volunteer and Employee Screening Guidebook," shares a range of tools guaranteed to help your screening efforts more closely match the position's responsibilities, below.

Source: Linda Graff, President, Linda Graff And Associates Inc., Dundas, Ontario, Canada. E-mail: Ll.Graff@sympatico.ca

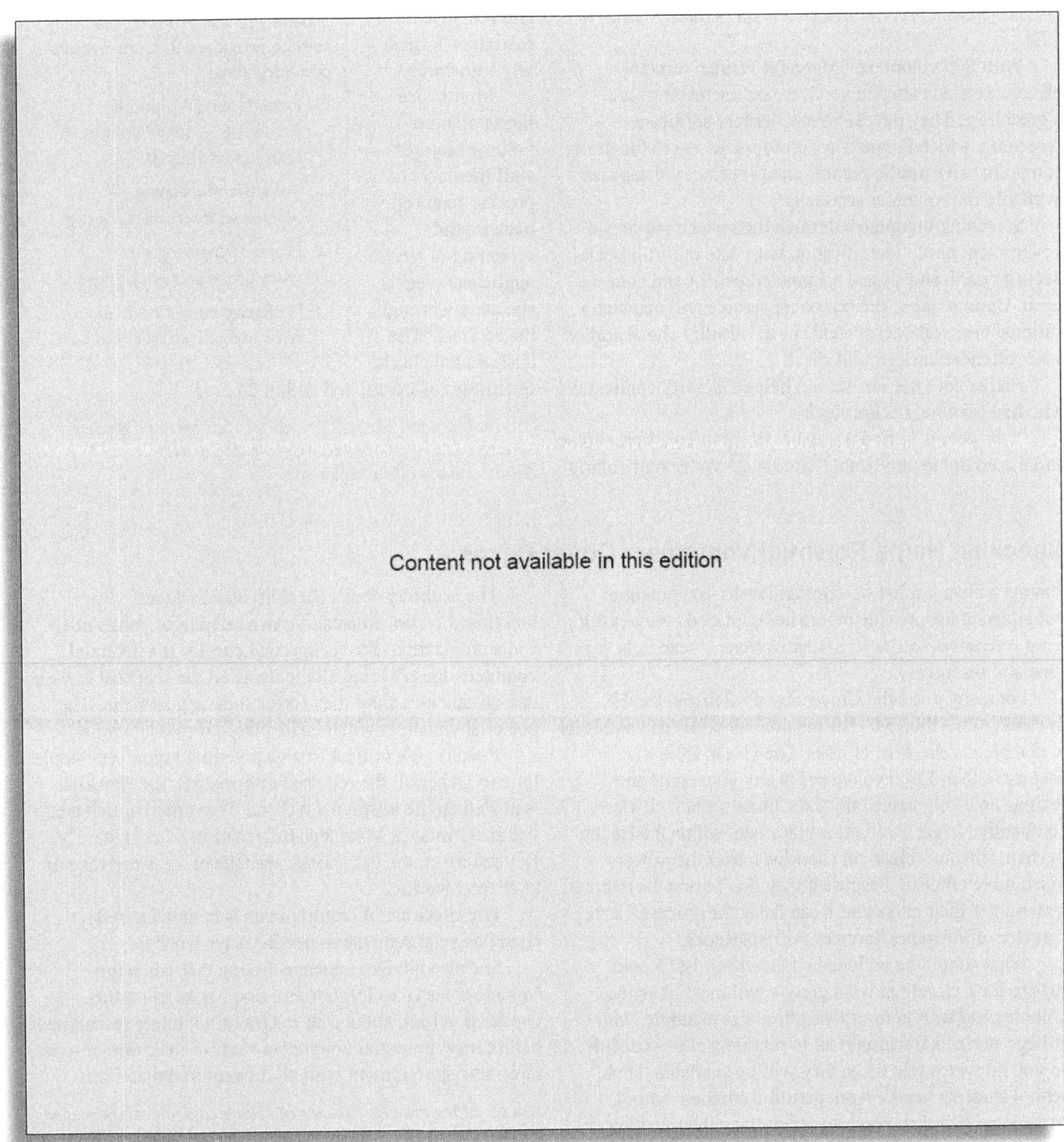

Services Help Simplify Volunteer Screening Process

Properly screening volunteers not only protects your organization and those it serves, it communicates to potential and current volunteers the responsibility of their role.

At Montefiore Medical Center (Bronx, NY), volunteer applicants are screened with the help of a service called Volunteer Screening, a nonprofit employee and volunteer background screening service of LexisNexis Company (Dayton OH).

With 800 volunteers, Margaret Hamer, director of volunteer and student services, says screenings are a great help. They pay $15 per volunteer applicant screening, which Hamer says provides access to the most comprehensive public records and proprietary databases available for volunteer screening.

Screening volunteers through the service requires a government photo identification with date of birth, Social Security card, and signed acknowledgement and consent form. Upon request, the screening service will conduct a national criminal background check, identity check and/or a sex offender background check.

Hamer says the service has helped identify applicants who had criminal backgrounds.

"Our goal is to find a suitable fit for the medical center and the volunteer applicant," she says. "We're particularly careful to identify those that have not fully disclosed all criminal background on their application, have entered false information or forged any signatures."

Montefiore's high volunteer volume requires staff members to process required background screening of new applicants weekly, she adds. Through the service, "The background check, oftentimes, is completed within 24 hours."

A Sampling of Screening Services

Volunteer screening services search national databases to identify applicants who have a criminal background. Here are four of the many service providers that offer volunteer screening:

- ☐ Lexis Nexis® Volunteer Screening — http://volunteer.lexisnexis.com/pub/
- ☐ Volunteer Screening — www.volunteerscreening.org
- ☐ Prehire Screening — www.prehirescreening.com
- ☐ My Background Check — www.mybackgroundcheck.com

Source: Margaret Hamer, Director of Volunteer and Student Services, Montefiore Medical Center, Bronx, NY.
E-mail: mhamer@montefiore.org

Checklist Helps Potential Volunteers Cover Bases

Having a clear cut list of items and tasks that potential volunteers must provide before being placed — everything from references to IDs to immunizations — can help save time and resources.

For many years the University of Michigan Health System (Ann Arbor, MI) has required all potential volunteers to complete a checklist of tasks. The Health System uses more than 1,600 volunteers at any given time and recruits new volunteers only three times a year. "It's very competitive to get a volunteer placement within the Health System. Having a clear-cut checklist makes the process much more efficient, because if they don't bring the required materials to their interview, it can delay the process," says Director of Volunteer Services, Alfreda Rooks.

What should be included on the checklist? Rooks says to look closely at what groups will most likely be volunteering with your organization. For example, with college students it's important to require a class schedule, so you know exactly when they will be available. High school students need a work permit from their school, and a legal guardian needs to accompany them to their interview.

The health system's checklist also includes immunization documentation, two references, forms of ID and authorizations for background checks. If a potential volunteer doesn't bring all the items on the checklist to their one-on-one interview, they forfeit their appointment. The potential volunteer will then be placed on a waiting list.

Because it's critical to give potential volunteers ample time to gather all the required information, the checklist is posted on the hospital's website (www.med.umich.edu/volunteer/images/Volunteer-Information-Checklist.pdf). Depending on the list, Rooks says the process can take up to several weeks.

The checklist of requirements is updated to reflect changing requirements as needed, says Rooks.

She also advises patience, noting that when the Volunteer Services Department first began using the checklist, it took about four cycles of volunteer recruitment before most potential volunteers came to their one-on-one interview appointment with all the required materials.

Source: Alfreda Rooks, Director of Volunteer Services, University of Michigan Health System, Ann Arbor, MI.
E-mail: arooks@umich.edu

Add a Skills Questionnaire to Your Volunteer Application

Most volunteer applications ask for personal information, education, work history and references. Going a step further, the volunteer application for Lee Memorial Health System (Fort Myers, FL), includes a skills questionnaire.

> "We capture more skills by using the checklist than by asking volunteers to write in their skills."

The questionnaire "enables us to capture the skills that each volunteer has, allowing us to create a large database of skills to pull from when needed," says Donna Bradish, director of volunteer resources. "If we need a photographer to cover an event, we query the database for the skill of photography and locate all the volunteers with this skill."

Shown below, the one-page questionnaire is divided into nine main categories, with check boxes for professional skills such as management, bookkeeping and customer relations, as well as more personal skills such as acting and gardening.

"We capture more skills by using the checklist than by asking volunteers to write in their skills," Bradish says. She says the only downside of the questionnaire is the tedious job of entering the skills into the database.

Source: Donna Bradish, Director of Volunteer Resources, Lee Memorial Hospital, Fort Myers, FL. E-mail: donna.bradish@leememorial.org

Content not available in this edition

Providing a list of skills that you are looking for is a better use of everyone's time.

Ask the Right Questions to Find Your Volunteer's Niche

Matching volunteers' skills, talents and preferences with their assignments is an effective way to maximize their potential and keep them coming back.

JoAnne Burris, volunteer coordinator, Cardinal Hill Rehabilitation Hospital (Lexington, KY), learns the skills of her 110 volunteers to determine how they can best help the staff and patients at the 108-bed hospital.

What's her secret? She simply asks the right questions.

Burris shares some questions she poses to volunteers to choose job assignments:

- What are you passionate about?
- What is/was your career and your greatest strength?
- What are you doing when you're the happiest?
- What task would you dread doing?
- (Once the volunteer has identified an area of interest or a specific project to take on, ask:) What is your vision of this project?

Through this interaction, Burris is better able to assign tasks, as well as recruit additional volunteers. For example, hospital volunteer Sharon Bennett, a master gardener assigned to work in the therapeutic garden used by the hospital's clients, recruited two other master gardeners to join her in the project.

"This idea bloomed, if you will," Burris says. "We not only benefitted from her passion for gardening, but also her networking skills when she identified others who would enjoy working to improve the therapeutic garden."

The questions also helped Burris put the talents of Cathy Boggs a retired schoolteacher to better use. Boggs decorated the hospital's pediatric center and waiting room to make them more comfortable and stimulating for young patients. And each month, she creates a colorful bulletin board and handouts filled with activity ideas for children.

The questions are just one way Burris seeks to understand what motivates her volunteers to give of their time. Those reasons vary for each one, she says: "Some people want to volunteer to get away from their daily job, and some have been away from it long enough and want a taste of it, but not do it full time. So (volunteering in a field in which they have experience) is a really nice balance."

Source: JoAnne Burris, Volunteer Coordinator, Cardinal Hill Rehabilitation Hospital, Lexington, KY. E-mail: jbb1@cardinalhill.org

Placement Questionnaire Addresses Volunteer Satisfaction

You and your staff invest plenty of time and resources into recruiting and training volunteers. But what do you do to measure their satisfaction levels or address concerns?

Volunteer services staff with Saint Joseph Hospital (Lexington, KY) use a one-page placement questionnaire to measure how satisfied new volunteers are with their assignments. Jamine Hamner, volunteer coordinator, says they developed the form six years ago after realizing they rarely saw many volunteers once they began volunteering, either because of the placement location or the volunteer's shift.

Hamner mails or e-mails the placement questionnaire, shown here, with a cover letter to volunteers two months into an assignment. She reviews responses and forwards them to the director or unit manager to which the volunteer is assigned.

"If a volunteer is not happy with his or her placement, we can notify the staff, so they can work with the volunteer to make the placement better, or we can reassign the volunteer to a more suitable placement," she says.

She estimates her office sends 300 questionnaires annually and sees about half returned, noting that the use of e-mail has resulted in a slight increase in returns.

Source: Jamine Hamner, Coordinator, Volunteer Services, Saint Joseph Hospital, Lexington, KY. E-mail: hamnerja@sjhlex.org

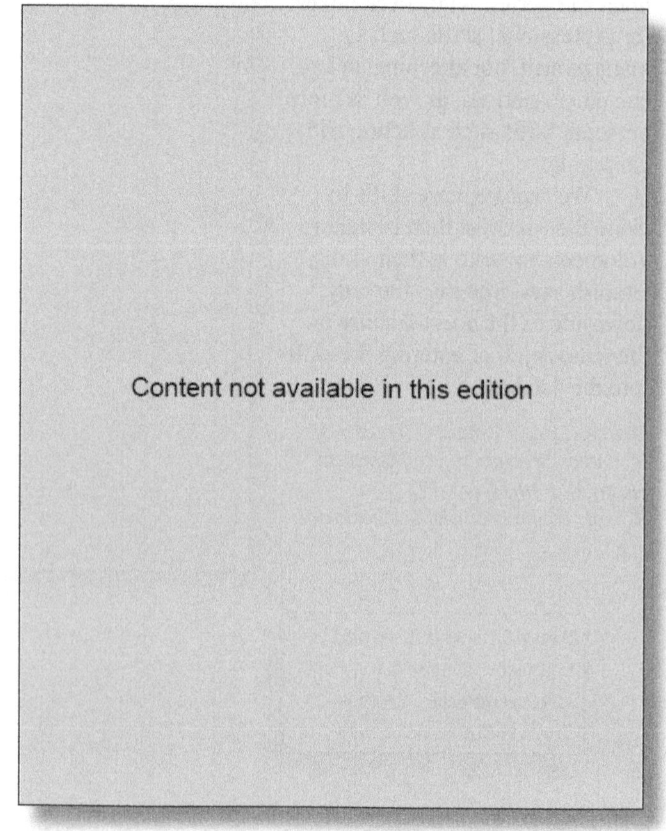

Content not available in this edition

© 2012 Stevenson, Inc. Published 2012 by Stevenson, Inc.

There are a variety of teaching/training methods you can use to increase volunteers' understanding of your organization, its work and its specific job duties. Education can even begin prior to a would-be volunteer accepting an appointment with your hospital or health organization. Although up-front training is essential, ongoing education is equally important and should not be overlooked.

Vary Teaching Styles to Offer Well-rounded Training

Consider using multiple teaching styles to help volunteers-in-training remain engaged and retain more of the important information they need to assist your organization and its mission.

At Fox Valley Volunteer Hospice (FVVH) of Geneva, IL, persons can expect a variety of teaching styles during their training sessions to help them prepare as thoroughly as possible for the often-emotional tasks involved with volunteering at the organization.

Training as an FVVH bereavement volunteer requires more than 20 hours of intensive training to learn the unique aspects of serving and supporting individuals and families who have experienced the death of a loved one, says Elise C. Wall, manager of volunteer services. Bereavement volunteers not only need to have compassion, Wall says, they need to learn skills in discussing grief, death and dying, to listen without judgment and to maintain personal boundaries.

Topics covered during training at FVVH include normal adult and children's grief, complicated grief, good communication skills with an emphasis on listening, self-care for both client and volunteer, exploring grief theories and preventing volunteer burnout.

To best cover this extensive list of complicated topics, Wall says, bereavement training includes a variety of teaching and learning styles to assist new volunteers with retention as follows:

- **Lectures.** Lectures can offer thorough details and explanations to volunteers, but can also be an area where volunteers can lose information when their minds become inundated or overloaded. Be sure to break lecture training up with frequent breaks, as well as small group discussions and role-playing. Create handouts with bullet points of critical information that will allow volunteers the opportunity to later review material covered.
- **Small group discussions.** Break volunteers into small groups of five or fewer to review accompanying lecture materials or to personalize the information covered based on their experiences as part of the layering process that will help them retain information.
- **Role playing.** Offer role-playing to allow volunteers to put the training into action and affirm what they have learned. Ask trainers and seasoned volunteers to role-play with trainees to ensure their understanding of material covered.
- **On-site training.** Create opportunities for recent volunteers to put their new knowledge into play within your organization by offering on-site training. Either pair new volunteers together or ask them to shadow experienced volunteers to witness training techniques in action.

Teach Effective Listening

A key component to offering effective support to clients facing the death of a loved one is the art of effective listening. In bereavement training, volunteers at the Fox Valley Volunteer Hospice (Geneva, IL) learn to listen effectively.

Elise C. Wall, manager of volunteer services, shares techniques they use, which can also help your volunteers to become more effective listeners:

- ✓ Listening with the intent to understand rather than with the intent to respond.
- ✓ Using open body language (e.g., arms and legs uncrossed).
- ✓ Maintaining eye contact with the client.
- ✓ Staying focused on the client, not allowing the mind to wander.
- ✓ Affirming the client's words with a nod.
- ✓ Being comfortable with silence, allowing the client to process his/her thoughts.
- ✓ Avoiding jumping to conclusions.

Source: Elise C. Wall, Manager of Volunteer Services, Fox Valley Volunteer Hospice, Geneva, IL. E-mail: ewall@fvvh.org

Volunteer Information Sessions Help Educate, Recruit

Whet potential volunteers' appetites with an upbeat, brief information session about helping your cause.

Five years ago, the Vanderbilt University Medical Center (Nashville, TN) began offering volunteer information sessions as a starting point for some of its 650 existing volunteers as well as persons interested in volunteering at the Monroe Carell Jr. Children's Hospital at Vanderbilt, Vanderbilt Medical Center and Vanderbilt Health – One Hundred Oaks, says Stephanie VanDyke, director of volunteer services at Monroe Carell Jr. Children's Hospital at Vanderbilt.

> Providing multiple opportunities for candidates and volunteers to gain a clearer perspective on institutional values allows you to develop a more cohesive team.

VanDyke says the sessions showcase hospital values, expectations and specific volunteer openings. In addition, they help educate potential volunteers about duties and expectations, and reduce costs for volunteer training by helping match recruits to appropriate volunteer tasks.

The training sessions feature a 15-minute video with interviews from current volunteers, an overview of the hospital and a look at the commitment and training that goes with being a hospital volunteer.

The one-hour sessions are offered one evening a month in January, March, May, August and September. VanDyke and Andrew Peterson, director of volunteer services at the adult hospital and clinics, say they see the highest attendance in August and September because many college students are available then. January is also another popular month because many people sign up to volunteer during the holiday season.

Interested volunteers are required to attend the information sessions and must register in advance. Peterson says they advertise the information sessions on the Vanderbilt website about four weeks before the session date. Posting the information any earlier, he says, can result in many people signing up, but then forgetting or losing interest. He adds that they have found that directing people to their website is the best way to advertise an upcoming session.

After the session, the attendees are given the opportunity to sign up for an interview, with about 90 percent of them doing so. Once the interview is complete, Vanderbilt works to have the new recruits in place within three to four weeks.

With the large number of interested volunteers, space limitations and the desire to follow-up and schedule interviews in a 3- to 4-week time frame, organizers limit the number of attendees at each session. While some sessions have seen more than 100 people sign up, on average Vanderbilt has 50 to 60 people register for each session.

Sources: Andrew Peterson, Director of Volunteer Services, Vanderbilt Medical Center, Nashville, TN.
E-mail: andrew.r.peterson@Vanderbilt.Edu
Stephanie VanDyke, Director, Volunteer Services, Monroe Carell Jr. Children's Hospital at Vanderbilt, Nashville, TN.
E-mail: stephanie.vandyke@Vanderbilt.Edu

Educate Volunteers With Impactful PowerPoint Presentations

Many nonprofit organizations rely on Microsoft PowerPoint presentations to educate audiences — including potential and current volunteers — about their cause. One such organization is the March of Dimes Michigan Chapter (Portage, MI). Dana DeLuca, the chapter's division director, offers six keys to creating effective presentations:

- Begin with an outline of what the audience will see and hear, then stick to it. Use the slides to clearly indicate where you are within the prepared outline.
- Keep the slides simple. Do not clutter them with too much information or hard-to-read text. If a slide is difficult to read, it is too busy or the font is too small.
- Keep the message simple and concise. Avoid covering a multitude of topics during one presentation.
- Keep the slides uniform in terms of design and format. Avoid changing color schemes and fonts and limit the frequency of moving from slide to slide.
- Utilize your nonprofit's colors and logos throughout the presentation to create brand identity and recognition.
- End with a summary of the key points and remind the audience of what was seen and heard during your presentation.

Source: Dana DeLuca, Division Director, March of Dimes, Portage, MI. E-mail: ddeluca@marchofdimes.com

Volunteer Training Addresses Language Challenges

If you're unable to read English, going to a hospital may be a struggle. That's why at Gouverneur Healthcare Services (New York, NY) special volunteers help patients understand basic medical instructions.

Volunteers with the Patient Navigation Program guide patients to their appointments and help them with tasks like signing up for a health plan, filling prescriptions and getting lab work done. "We let them know that when they are navigating a patient, they essentially are adding to that patient's experience and helping to form an impression of our facility," says Carolyn Bachino, program director of the Volunteerism and Health Literacy Program.

All volunteers with the Patient Navigation Program go through a specialized seven-hour training session. The volunteers are taught to use the teach-back method of communication to ensure that patients understand the instructions they are given. They are also taught how to:

- Read, understand and communicate medical instructions and information. "We sensitize them to the fact that the majority of our patients here do not know how to read and/or write English, but that it has no bearing on their intelligence," says Bachino.
- Talk to patients about Ask Me 3 — a patient education program designed to promote communication between health care providers and patients.
- Keep a medication log to track a patient's medications.
- Navigate patients around the building.
- Keep logs indicating how they helped each patient.

The training also uses a picture book called 'At the Doctor's Office' to give volunteers a taste of what it's like to negotiate a medical visit in an unfamiliar language. The book features captions written entirely in code, and volunteers are given ten minutes to decode the messages and explain the story. "We have found this to be a very eye-opening exercise for many of the volunteers," says Bachino.

Volunteer training also includes role-playing exercises and a one- to seven-hour practicum with an experienced volunteer or staff member.

Sources: Carolyn Bachino, Program Director; William Calabrese, Director of Quality Management; Devika Nandlall, Program Coordinator, Volunteerism and Health Literacy Program, Gouverneur Healthcare Services, New York, NY.
E-mail: carolyn.bachino@nychhc.org, Devika.Nandlall@nychhc.org, William.Calabrese@nychhc.org

Training Gift Shop Volunteers

Train gift shop volunteers the same way as you would paid employees: Provide them with customer service training; make sure they know the shop's policies and procedures; and continually remind them of the importance of making customers feel welcome.

Nancy Cerqueira, director of volunteer services, W. A. Foote Memorial Hospital (Jackson, MI), oversees the hospital's 1,700-square-foot gift shop, which is operated by 40 volunteers and brings in $500,000 annually.

Cerqueira recruits and interviews candidates who possess people skills, sales experience and an interest in the job.

Her training includes:

1. **An orientation covering customer service.** Cerqueira bases the training on the acronym, AIDET:
   - **A:** Acknowledge the customer
   - **I.** Introduce self to customer
   - **D.** Duration of time to help the customer
   - **E:** Exclamation, which includes helping the customer, and
   - **T:** Thanking the customer.
2. **One-on-one training with the gift shop coordinator.** The coordinator covers the training manual, which includes hospital history, safety procedures, position descriptions, daily cleaning checklists, a buying guide, plus policies on appearance, scheduling and forms.
3. **On-the-job training.** Volunteers learn from hands-on demonstrations to operate the cash register, process credit card transactions, make payroll deductions and more.

Source: Nancy Cerqueira, Director, Volunteer Services, W.A. Foote Memorial Hospital, Jackson, MI.
E-mail: nancy.cerqueira@wafoote.org

Select Supplemental Training Programs for Volunteers

Finding the proper training program for your volunteers can pay off in countless ways.

Sarah Ferro, volunteer coordinator at Hospice of St. Tammany (Mandeville, LA), did extensive research to determine the best training program for her hospice volunteers. Her choice: "My Gift: Myself," a volunteer training program specifically for hospice volunteers.

Ferro shares steps other volunteer managers can take to determine what training program would work best for their organization and its volunteers:

- ✓ **Evaluate training programs based on specificity and needs.** Develop a list that spells out current training needs and use that to research training programs that will best fulfill those requirements. When evaluating "My Gift: Myself," Ferro found that the package contained seven DVDs that covered the history of hospice, listening skills, physical care, spiritual needs for hospice families, understanding bereavement, volunteer self-preservation and volunteer activities.
- ✓ **Refine your budget.** Determine that the training program offers you the most bang for your buck. Many training program websites include cost analysis functions to aid in evaluating cost.
- ✓ **Evaluate the printed materials — including manuals, quizzes and leader materials — that will accompany the computer-based training.** Have qualified staff and volunteers review the printed materials to evaluate the level of training provided. Ferro's decision to purchase "My Gift: Myself" was partially based on the program's design to incorporate printed materials. During the DVD presentation, the program pauses at relevant points to allow trainees to complete printed workbook pages. Check for and review leaders' materials to ensure that they will help develop solutions to questions/problems throughout training.
- ✓ **Request trial materials or samples to determine if the training is best geared to your needs.** Ask seasoned volunteers to evaluate the trial materials and its effectiveness before purchasing.
- ✓ **Create an evaluation form** for staff and seasoned volunteers to complete in order to rate each training package.

Source: Sarah S. Ferro, Office/Volunteer Coordinator, Hospice of St. Tammany, Mandeville, LA. E-mail: sferro@stph.org

Prepare Volunteers for Emotional Turmoil

When someone volunteers to be with a patient who is dying, it can be an emotionally challenging task. For volunteers performing such services, being emotionally strong is critical. In addition to the standard volunteer training, special trainings on death and dying can be very important.

> Proactive connections with front line volunteers show your commitment to them and gives them the opportunity to share their concerns.

No One Dies Alone (NODA) is a program that provides companionship for dying patients who have no family or friends nearby. At Sacred Heart Medical Center (Eugene, OR) — the organization at which the program was launched — NODA volunteers go through a six- to eight-hour training that includes:

- An introduction to the program and the role of the compassionate companion.
- What to do when you get the phone call, such as where to go, what to wear and how to get an escort if it's after hours.
- What to expect for yourself, both emotionally and spiritually.
- What physically will happen to patients as they die.
- What is and isn't helpful to a dying patient.

Carleen McCornack, NODA program coordinator at Sacred Heart, is in charge of calling volunteers when a patient is nearing death. "When I call a NODA volunteer, I tell them we are activating a vigil and ask if they have any time available in the next two days to come and sit at a bedside. This way if they are not emotionally up to it or busy at the time I'm calling, they can let me know a time that would work better for them," she says.

Typically vigils last two to three days, but each volunteer sits with the patient for no more than four hours. Following each vigil, McCornack follows up with the volunteers who were involved. "Ongoing and open communication is key. After the vigil is over I thank them for their support with either a phone call or a handwritten note. If the volunteer says they need additional counseling or spiritual guidance, I can direct them to someone who can help," she says.

Since these volunteers are used on an as-needed basis, Clarke suggests keeping in touch with all the volunteers via e-mail about once a week, so they know that even though they weren't needed that week, they are still valued.

Source: Carleen McCornack, No One Dies Alone Program Coordinator, Sacred Heart Medical Center, Eugene, OR. E-mail: cmccornack@peacehealth.org

Tasks Require In-depth Training

At Houston Hospice (Houston, TX), volunteers are required to attend 25 hours of training in order to prepare to work with people with chronic or terminal illnesses.

"Our training covers hospice basics, grief and loss, listening skills, social, spiritual and medical aspects of care," says Ruth Landauer, director of volunteer services. "It provides volunteers with information about hospice services and the dying process, as well as the training they need to comfortably visit with patients and families.

"A large part of our training is to help volunteers better understand their own grief experiences and develop good listening skills," Landauer says. "By the end of the training, they understand that they don't have the answers to the issues facing our patients and families; it is their presence that matters — the key to successful hospice work. Twenty-five hours of training also gives us the opportunity to get to know the volunteers well."

Training involves group activities, lectures, videos and group discussions.

Because of the responsibility that comes with hospice volunteering, she says, "Our training is more comprehensive in covering the issues we consider necessary to successful volunteering. I believe it is our responsibility to see that volunteers have the skills and information they need before they visit with hospice families."

Training classes typically include 15 to 30 participants. They are offered three times a year in classroom settings, with self-study available as needed.

> Standardized training prepares all volunteers for the work regardless of previous experience.

How do volunteers react to that training time requirement?

"The people who are looking for quality hospice training appreciate our training because they recognize how unprepared they are to provide comfort to patients and families without this type of in-depth training," Landauer says. "Many people come to our training, rather than other hospices, because they have heard about it from others. A self-study program is available for those who do not want to attend the sessions. We also welcome members of the community to attend the classes for educational purposes."

Sources: Ruth Landauer, Director of Volunteer Services, and Cynthia Nordt, Interim Vice President of Development, Houston Hospice, Houston, TX. E-mail: cnordt@houstonhospice.org

Get Fresh Ideas for In-service Training Topics

Coming up with new and different topics for your continuing education events each year can be challenging. Here's how one volunteer manager keeps trainings fresh:

After 10 years in volunteer management, Jennifer Thompson, coordinator, volunteer and family services, Good Shepherd Hospice (Tulsa, OK), says she was running low on ideas for in-service training programs. So she turned to her volunteers for help.

"Not only do I get new ideas, but when they come up with their own ideas, it gives them ownership of the volunteer program, and they're more likely to stay on," Thompson says.

The volunteer coordinator sets the year's first in-service training as a mandatory annual meeting. All of the hospice's volunteers — numbering two dozen — attend, eagerly brainstorming ideas for the six to eight in-service trainings they'll have that year.

Thompson says she leads and guides them, but the volunteers themselves come up with topics they would like to see covered. Some of the volunteer-chosen in-service topics include pet therapy and learning the friends approach when dealing with Alzheimer's patients.

An added benefit of involving volunteers is that the volunteers can help reduce presentation costs by making presentations themselves.

> Providing volunteers with what they are looking for enriches their volunteer experience and provides then with valuable knowledge.

Thompson says one of her volunteers was also a docent at an art museum, and she suggested a visit to a Native American exhibit to look at the topic of death and dying as portrayed in various art forms.

Thompson says other volunteers will tape television programs that deal with hospice issues, and the volunteers will all watch the programs together for a film night.

Source: Jennifer Thompson, CVA, Coordinator of Volunteer and Family Services, Good Shepherd Hospice — Tulsa, Tulsa, OK. E-mail: Jennifer.Thompson@goodshepherdhospices.com

Tip to Reinforce Training

You've heard of a suggestion box, but how about a competency box?

Heather Powers, volunteer coordinator, Condell Medical Center Hospice (Libertyville, IL), uses a competency box at roundtable meetings with volunteers. The box is filled with questions based on volunteer continuing education training as well as situational problems.

During the meetings, a volunteer pulls out a question and tries to answer it in front of the group. Powers says it's a great way to engage volunteers, offer praise for right answers and correct misconceptions.

Heather Powers, Volunteer Coordinator, Condell Medical Center Hospice, Libertyville, IL. E-mail: hpowers@condell.org

Eliminate Future Confusion: Give Mentors a Checklist During Training

Mentors require extensive training to be able to handle the numerous situations that can arise working with volunteers and clients.

Debra Tucker, volunteer coordinator, Pregnancy Care Center (Springfield, MO), found many of her organization's mentors had numerous questions about their duties even after being trained. To help eliminate some of those questions and allow both volunteers and staff to feel more comfortable with the training, she created a three-page Mentor Training Checklist.

Checklists are a valuable tool for helping mentors/trainers. This helps to avoid missed lessons while on boarding new volunteers.

Volunteers, staff and Tucker all gave input as to what to include.

Shown in part at right, the checklist includes items volunteer mentors need to complete before starting on their own. The checklist is given to the volunteers once they arrive for training. Tasks can be completed at the volunteer's own pace, but Tucker says staff encourages them to complete training and start volunteering as soon as they are able. Once they complete the checklist, it is reviewed by a staff supervisor.

Tucker says that besides offering a more complete training procedure, the checklist allows trainees to feel confident that when they have completed the list of requirements, they are better qualified to handle the position.

In addition to completing the checklist volunteers shadow train with other mentors.

The organization's mentors serve as confidantes to pregnant women and provide support and resources to expectant mothers, fathers and parents.

Source: Debra Tucker, Volunteer Coordinator, Pregnancy Care Center, Springfield, MO.
E-mail: volunteers@pccchoices.org

A comprehensive mentor checklist, shown in part here, helps guarantee volunteers with the Pregnancy Care Center (Springfield, MO) are trained for and understand their duties.

Content not available in this edition

© 2012 Stevenson, Inc. Published 2012 by Stevenson, Inc.

In addition to education and training procedures, the ways in which you nurture volunteers — both one-on-one and in group situations — will impact your ability to motivate and retain them for long periods of time. While not all forms of volunteering can be labeled as fun, the experience should be fulfilling. Your caring acts of kindness will go far in keeping volunteers energized and eager to take on future projects.

Timely, Friendly Contact Key to Recruitment

Making your volunteers feel appreciated from the first contact they have with your organization is critical to maintaining a roster of good Samaritans ready to pitch in at all times.

No one knows that better than Suz McIver, director of volunteers at Midland Care (Topeka, KS). Because Midland Care volunteers deal with hospice patients, McIver says, burnout is a frequent problem, creating a constant need for new volunteers. She handles this by streamlining the process of welcoming new volunteers into the organization.

"The challenge is to get volunteer help in there as soon as we can," McIver says.

The effort to secure new volunteers is a team effort between McIver, a part-time staff member and a part-time clerical volunteer. They mail information packets to potential volunteers within 24 hours of initial contact and follow up with a phone call within a week. Next, McIver interviews the volunteers for placement. Persons who are brought on as volunteers undergo extensive training in sessions offered every three months.

McIver's advice for successful volunteer recruitment is to be flexible about volunteer opportunities and schedules. For example, Midland Care operates a resale store that volunteers may staff, if they prefer to not work directly with patients. The organization also offers volunteer shifts on nights and weekends.

In addition, McIver recommends being open during the orientation process, so that volunteer candidates know what to expect and can walk away if it's not for them.

Midland Care currently has 167 active volunteers and averages five volunteer inquiries each week, says McIver, who credits this high response to community awareness about Midland Care's mission, vision and values.

Source: Suz McIver, Director of Volunteers, Midland Care, Topeka, KS. E-mail: smciver@midlandcc.org

Personal Phone Calls Build Rapport With Volunteers

Coming into a volunteer management position when the person you're replacing was well-loved can be difficult. Lakeesha Campbell, volunteer coordinator, Presbyterian Hospice and Palliative Care (Charlotte, NC), has a simple, proven way to build rapport:

Every two weeks, Campbell calls each of her 50 volunteers. She keeps calls low key and personal, asking how the volunteer is and if he/she needs anything from her.

Campbell says her predecessor advised her to make the calls to build and maintain personal relationships with the volunteers. She admits that at first she thought there was no way she could find time for 50 personal phone calls every other week. But, by splitting the list up and making about 10 calls a day, she can do so easily.

The personal calls let Campbell stay close with volunteers and offer a chance just to say, "Hello," rather than just calling when she has a volunteer need to fill.

Source: Lakeesha Campbell, Volunteer Coordinator, Presbyterian Hospice and Palliative Care, Charlotte, NC. E-mail: lcampbell@novanthealth.org

Liven Up Your Events With a Bit of Fun

Boost your volunteers' spirits and liven up your events by adding a bit of fun.

"Injecting lighthearted humor can brighten and lift the spirits through healthy laughter," says Mary Maxted, volunteer coordinator, Hospice of Washington County (Washington, IA). She notes that adding fun to volunteer events is especially beneficial for organizations such as hospice that focus on a serious subject.

Maxted shares three techniques she uses with her volunteers.

> Functions that personalize the administrative processes add tremendous value and increase volunteer commitment. They also may help your program stand out if an individual is considering more than one organization for a volunteer opportunity.

- **Get-acquainted Exercise:** When working with a group of new volunteers, have them write their names on index cards, adding a word that describes their personality and begins with the first letter of their first name (e.g., Cindy-creative; Beth-banker). Have them share their names and descriptive word with each other.
- **Fun Awards:** In addition to traditional volunteer awards, Maxted mixes in fun awards (e.g., giving Superman T-shirts to volunteers with "super" powers).
- **Entertainment:** Maxted invites local vocal ensembles to volunteer functions.

Source: Mary Maxted, Volunteer Coordinator, Hospice of Washington County, Washington, IA.
E-mail: volunteercoord@hospicewashingtoncounty.org

Newsletter Gives Volunteers, Others, Glimpse Inside Nonprofit

Communicating with volunteers through a volunteer newsletter has become a critical key to the success of the volunteer program at Cook Children's Health Care System (Fort Worth, TX), says Marie Howell, volunteer program manager.

Using these tools to illustrate the impact that volunteers have means that the newsletter can serve double duty as a marketing tool.

One important role the newsletter plays, Howell says, is to share photos and information of volunteer events. The newsletter also covers events going on outside of the volunteer department to keep volunteers in the know within the nonprofit.

Howell shares insight on how to create an effective volunteer newsletter or revamp an existing one to better serve your volunteer corps:

- **Take photos of your organization's events.** Share the photos so that volunteers who do not attend can get a feel for the event, says Howell. "We make sure our events and gatherings range from the casual to the semi formal, from light-hearted themes to more formal presentations, from just-for-fun to educational," says Howell. "In that way, we try to have something for every taste and age at least a couple times a year, with the realization that you can't please everyone. The volunteers give us a lot of positive feedback on the newsletter."
- **Feature photos and information about what is going on outside the volunteer department.** "Recently, Cook Children's launched a line of patient art-inspired gifts and collectibles for sale on our website," she says. "The only way the volunteers could know about it was through the newsletter. In fact, we got the scoop on the product launch so they found out about it before it was announced to paid staff! The newsletter also keeps them up to speed anytime Cook Children's receives national recognition, an award, or opens a new facility. It's important that they be a part of the whole picture."
- **Keep it simple and share it with volunteers and staff.** "Our newsletter is very simple but very popular," says Howell. "In fact, we had a contest in which the volunteers named the newsletter several years ago, so it is truly theirs. We also send the newsletter to the volunteer supervisors so they stay up to speed."

Source: Marie Howell, Volunteer Program Manager, Cook Children's Health Care System, Fort Worth, TX. E-mail: marie.howell@cookchildrens.org

Maximize Website Message

While volunteer newsletters remain a mainstay in communicating with your volunteer corps (see main story, left), virtual methods of communication continue to grow as a means to recruit volunteers.

At Cook Children's Health Care System (Fort Worth, TX), officials intentionally redesigned its volunteer Web page to attract the attention of current and potential volunteers. Here, Marie Howell, volunteer program manager, shares three tips for revamping your volunteer Web page to get more volunteer attention:

1. Update your organization's home page so that persons who visit it immediately see the word volunteer. "This was a huge change as we had been buried before under the weight of many drop-down menus," says Howell. "We noticed an immediate increase in applications from the website."
2. Create a strong relationship with your webmaster. This allows you freedom to try new things on your website and realize the potential of what you may be able to do.
3. Encourage prospective volunteers to visit your website to learn about your agency, its history, plans, volunteer program and more. There's only so much information you can give during an interview or phone call.

Celebrate Volunteers' Birthdays

At the Mississippi Valley Regional Blood Center (MVRBC) of Davenport, IA, each of the 400 volunteers receives a special honor once a year in the form of a birthday card.

"This is a simple gesture from the company to say, 'Happy birthday, and have a great day,'" says Kay Parch, manager of volunteer relations. Cards are signed "MVRBC" so recipients know they come from the entire blood center staff.

To honor your volunteers, Parch says:

- ✓ Consider purchasing discounted cards in bulk. Parch buys cards from It Takes Two (www.ittakestwo.com), a Minnesota-based company that specializes in wholesale greeting cards for volunteers, at a cost of $1 a card.
- ✓ Create a fund or budget item that will fund the cards and postage. If budget is a concern, consider hand-delivering cards to volunteers during their volunteer shifts on or around their birthdays.
- ✓ Consider sending e-mail greetings from services such as Blue Mountain where, for a minimal membership fee, cards can be sent via e-mail. Most such companies offer free trial periods.
- ✓ Find a greeting card supplier or online service that lets you plug dates into an online calendar and sends you e-mail reminders of the impending day.

Source: Kay Parch, Manager of Volunteer Relations, Mississippi Valley Regional Blood Center, Davenport, IA. E-mail: kparch@mvrbc.com

Tips for Staffing Your Hospital Gift Shop

Are you doing all you can to keep your volunteers motivated?

Patricia Sterner incorporates fun and prizes into her management of volunteers at the University of Iowa Hospital Clinics Wild Rose Gifts (Iowa City, IA).

"Our director has encouraged us to give lots of praise and also give treats or gift certificates for good customer service or other behavior," Sterner says. "We actually have a written definition of customer service, and when we hear our volunteers using specific language relating to it, we do want to encourage it more."

To keep volunteers motivated, Sterner says she is always looking for contests with prizes. She even uses this concept to improve gift shop management techniques. For example, when the volunteer manager found that a clipboard that is used to record merchandise requests was not being used as much as intended, she hosted a name-the-clipboard contest. She plans to award the contest winner with a prize, "then put a big sign on the clipboard with the name," which she hopes will help volunteers remember to use this tool.

Sterner says that while she provides new volunteers with a volunteer handbook, she believes they learn better from watching and imitating staff behavior. She says gift shop managers also meet with their volunteers two or more times a year to review training and address concerns. "And once a year we try to have a party, no training, just fun!"

For Sterner, scheduling her 30 gift shop volunteers is simple: "Our volunteers work a specific time each week, for example, Monday mornings 9:30-12:30. Then I only have to find subs when they are absent."

Beyond scheduling and reward matters, finding the right volunteers — and working with them and their schedule outside of the gift shop — can make a major impact on their satisfaction and, ultimately, how long they stay with your organization.

Linda Dias coordinates gift shop volunteers at Butler Hospital (Providence, RI). She says many retirees enjoy volunteering at the gift shop because it fits well with their schedules. The Butler Hospital Gift Shop doesn't have a specific schedule for volunteers, Dias says. Rather, volunteers work when it works for them. "Some do four hours a week, others do full days, it all depends on the individual."

Sources: Linda Dias, Human Resource and Volunteer Coordinator, Butler Hospital, Providence, RI.
E-mail: ldias@butler.org
Patricia Sterner, UIHC Wild Rose Gifts, Iowa City, IA.
E-mail: patricia-sterner@uiowa.edu

Keep the Aging Volunteer as a Valuable Part of the Team

We all know the kind: senior volunteers who consistently show up every week, doing their work without question or fanfare. But how do you keep them engaged when age-related disabilities begin to interfere?

Lynne Hagmann, former operations coordinator, Make-A-Wish Foundation of Northeast New York (Cohoes, NY), says the value of these volunteers can far outweigh the challenges, if managed with care and compassion.

Hagmann advises keeping these tips in mind to keep aging volunteers involved:

- **Be patient.** You may need to explain things more slowly or several times.
- **Be consistent.** Changes in work environment can be upsetting to seniors.
- **Be flexible.** Change, while daunting, may be warranted (e.g., macular degeneration prevents computer work, Parkinson's tremors prevent stuffing envelopes and mailings). Try to find a task older volunteers can easily manage, so they can continue to be productive and helpful.
- **Organize work stations.** Make sure areas are well-lit and chairs are stable. Consider tools such as those used to magnify computer screens.
- **Educate others.** If a senior volunteer has a medical condition such as diabetes, make sure staff and other volunteers are alerted to recognize signs of trouble.

Last but not least, Hagmann says: "Take the time to learn about their lives and their work experiences. It is amazing what they can teach you."

Source: Lynne Hagmann, former Operations Coordinator, Make-A-Wish Foundation of Northeast New York, Cohoes, NY. E-mail: john2145@aol.com

Tips for Working With Seniors

Here are a few additional tips for successfully working with seniors at your nonprofit:

- ✓ Ask staffers to wear name tags and always introduce themselves at volunteer meetings to assist seniors (and others) in recall.
- ✓ Find out the volunteer's preferred method of communication. They may prefer written notes or phone calls.
- ✓ Learn physical activity levels they can easily accomplish. Some may prefer a seated task, while others can easily work on their feet.
- ✓ Ask about their former or current careers to identify the best way to involve them. Retired accountants, for example, may prefer to help with accounting or cash register tasks.
- ✓ Keep communication lines open. Check in frequently to ensure all is going well. Offer frequent breaks and opportunities to socialize with staffers and other volunteers.

Reduce Compassion Fatigue While Strengthening Resilience

If your organization's mission puts your volunteers, your staff, and even yourself into highly stressful situations, be on the lookout for signs of compassion fatigue.

Compassion fatigue is the extreme state experienced by those helping others in distress and preoccupation with the suffering of those they are helping to the point of traumatizing the volunteer or helper. It can be a common ailment among volunteers who work with clients dealing with traumatic events, health issues or animal welfare.

Kim Heinrichs, executive director of volunteer resources at San Diego Hospice and The Institute for Palliative Medicine (San Diego, CA), shares signs her organization uses to determine if someone is experiencing compassion fatigue:

- Inability to define healthy boundaries.
- Desire or need to fix patients' problems.
- Hesitation to share volunteer intervention with staff team members.
- Believing that patient can't survive without his/her help.
- Feeling of hopelessness as though nothing he/she does will make anything better.

Heinrichs shares steps to go from compassion fatigue to professional resilience:

- Take a break between patient or client assignments.
- Participate in supportive supervision meetings, volunteer continuing education and support from volunteer staff or coordinator.
- Discover and commit to personal self-care, including exercise, gardening, meditation or other forms of relaxation.
- Maintain open communication between volunteer and staff to tackle potential patient or family challenges before they become a problem.

"Managers must understand that burnout is real and exists for both volunteers and staff," Heinrichs says. "Commit to best training and support practices by using training modules, available from national organizations such as the National Hospice and Palliative Care Organization (Alexandria, VA) and Volunteering in America (Washington, D.C.)." She recommends training modules that incorporate key topics such as saying goodbye, compassionate listening, boundary issues and best practices to educate and support volunteers.

Finally, Heinrichs says, be approachable and understanding, so volunteers will seek help from the management team. Enforce clear, ongoing communication between volunteer coordinators by instituting check-in calls to facilitate safe, open dialogue.

Source: Kim Heinrichs, Executive Director of Volunteer Resources, San Diego Hospice and The Institute for Palliative Medicine, San Diego, CA. E-mail: KHeinrichs@SDHospice.org. Website: www.sdhospice.org

Volunteer Management Essentials for Hospitals & Health-Related Nonprofits.
Edited by Paul Bartush.
© 2012 Stevenson, Inc. Published 2012 by Stevenson, Inc.

What are you doing to attract and nuture youth as volunteers? What about interns? Are you being proactive in building a viable internship program at your hospital or health-related organization? Young people can provide valuable volunteer assistance while gaining personally in a number of ways. Take every opportunity to enlist and nurture young people in your volunteer programs.

Internships Give Volunteers Professional Career Options

Offer value-added opportunities such as internships as incentive for current volunteers to sign on for additional hours and newcomers to sign up to help your cause.

The Gaston Hospice and Grief Counseling Services (Gastonia, NC) partners with area nursing schools, universities and the local high school to offer internships to students interested in the fields of nursing, counseling and social work.

Interns take part in hands-on work with patients and gain significant career experience. For example, social work and counseling interns manage a caseload just like paid social workers or counselors, gaining a realistic idea of the profession's day-to-day obligations. These interns are supervised by the social work manager and director of counseling services. Counseling interns also work with community grief clients as well as hospice families.

Because of the internship program, Gaston Hospice has four nursing school student interns and four counseling and social work interns at any given time.

Jennifer Jones, volunteer coordinator, offers suggestions to provide successful internship opportunities for area students:

- ❑ First and foremost, be sure the clinical staff is on board with the partnership program and agreeable to working with interns. Gaston Hospice clinical staff recognize the inherent value of their interns and appreciate the additional assistance for the patients' well-being.
- ❑ Limit intern opportunities to a comfortable level where staff can handle additional efforts needed to manage intern staff and are also able to provide the appropriate environment for the interns to learn.
- ❑ Offer career opportunities to interns completing their coursework within your institution. Encourage interns who have worked within your organization to apply for long-term career positions. At Gaston Hospice, employment opportunities are listed at the hospital system's website and staff work with interns to offer them career placement within the organization.

> If you don't believe that you can support an internship program, consider soliciting support from long-term volunteers.

Source: Jennifer Jones, Volunteer Coordinator, Gaston Hospice and Grief Counseling Services, Gastonia, NC.
E-mail: cunningj@gmh.org

Volunteer Interview, Organization Foundation for Success

Kathryn Berry Carter, director of volunteer services at St. Jude Children's Research Hospital (Memphis, TN), encourages nonprofits to host interns as volunteers.

"Although an intern program takes time to manage, the outcomes are extremely positive and far more beneficial than the time expended," says Carter, whose department works with one to three interns each semester. The experience, she says, "can teach students so much about their likes and dislikes and, most importantly, give them a chance to gain confidence in your profession. Remind the students you interact with of these advantages and you will likely have no trouble recruiting."

If you have several applicants for a limited number of internships, conduct a formal interview process, asking behavioral and situational questions, similar to what paid employees must undergo, she says. This gives prospective students interview experience, while helping you find the candidate that best fits your needs. Involve the staff who will work most closely or even those who will supervise the intern in the selection process.

"Ensure that the projects your interns work on are well-documented for sustainability purposes, especially if the assignment will be carried from intern to intern," Carter says.

She also recommends providing an intern orientation process similar to a new employee orientation that educates interns on basic information, such as:

- ❑ Which meetings must they attend, and which ones can they skip?
- ❑ What is the process for calling in sick?
- ❑ How does the intern schedule a vacation day, and what steps do they need to take with the projects they are working on in anticipation of a vacation day?
- ❑ What is a typical daily work schedule?

Carter also recommends meeting with interns briefly at the start of their daily shifts to ensure that their priorities are in line with where you want them to expend their energies.

Ask interns to set goals and expectations at the beginning of the experience and review them mid-term and at the conclusion of the semester, she says. "This helps greatly to ensure the experience not only meets with their expectations, but also yours. You can guide and support and renegotiate assignments based on these guiding principles."

Finally, ask exiting interns for feedback — including what they felt went well and what didn't, plus suggestions for improvement — to help you refine your internship program.

Source: Kathryn Berry Carter, Director of Volunteer Services, St. Jude Children's Research Hospital, Memphis, TN
E-mail: Kathryn.Berry-Carter@Stjude.org

Organized Objectives Help Staff Buy In To Intern Program

One of the biggest concerns when creating an internship program is whether your staff will buy in to the project.

That concern is warranted, since your organization's staff will be the ones working directly with the interns, taking the time to teach them and allowing them to job shadow.

When Denise Lamphier, director, volunteer services, La Porte Regional Health System (La Porte, IN), created her VolunTeen student internship program (see brochure, below), she wanted to make sure the students, age 14 to 18, got an opportunity for a hands-on learning experience.

Twenty-seven hospital departments — from family practice to the cancer center to medical records — take part in the VolunTeen program. Throughout the school year, and during a special summer session, these departments allow a student to volunteer for four hours a week and see first-hand what they do.

To get staff from these departments to buy in to the project, Lamphier worked with one of the hospital's clinical educators to develop student objective sheets. Lamphier then worked with each department director to adjust objective sheets to specific departments.

With this tool in hand, she says, department staff knew how they were expected to interact with the students, and the students knew what to expect, as well.

Lamphier says the student objective sheets come in especially handy when a new staff person comes on who hasn't worked with the interns yet. The staff person can look at the objective sheet and know exactly what the intern can do or needs to do. She says both the staff and department directors feel more comfortable with the process.

Source: Denise Lamphier, Director Volunteer Services, La Porte Regional Health System, La Porte, IN. E-mail: d.lamphier@lph.org

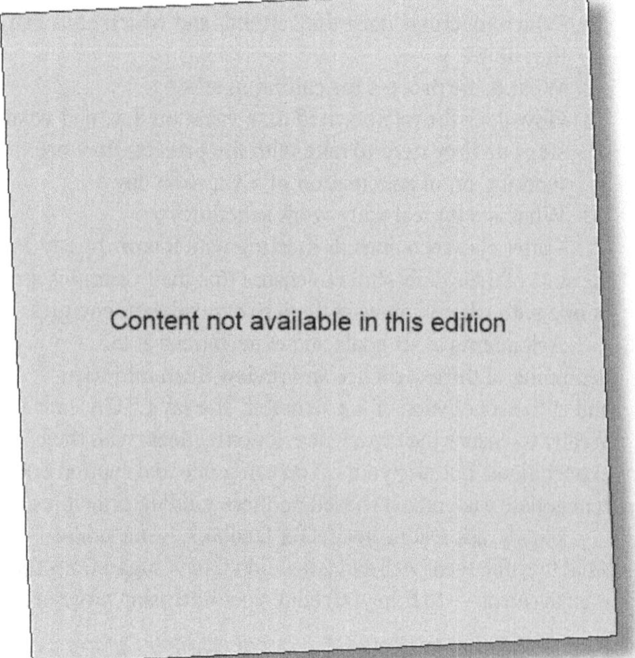

Content not available in this edition

Start at the Top for Staff Buy-in

Why don't staff buy in to the value of volunteers?

Perhaps they don't know volunteers' relevance to the organization. Maybe they're unsure what to do with volunteers or feel they infringe on staff duties. Whatever the reason, lack of buy-in of volunteers' value can lead to an underused program and poor volunteer retention rates.

Jennifer Gilligan Cole, president, Cole Community Concepts (Nashville, TN), says she has seen many volunteer managers try to fix volunteer/staff relations on a small level when the solution lies with an organization's top management.

To create staff buy-in, Cole says, ask your CEO and board to define volunteering. Do they know what type of strategic impact volunteers make? Approach upper management by showing them how volunteers fit into and enhance a successful business strategy.

First, show these key players how volunteers make a positive financial impact on the organization (e.g., What would happen to the organization if there were no volunteers? What wouldn't get done and what would have to be paid to higher staff to fill their roles?).

Secondly, consider the amount of staff time it actually takes to manage volunteers. Cole says she recently told a nonprofit's board its staff spend 30 percent of their time managing volunteers. The board had no idea and was shocked by this number.

Upper management needs to not only recognize the amount of time staff manages volunteers by giving them performance reviews and support, but also include that in the initial job description, so staff isn't caught off guard, she says. Once you emphasize to upper management just how critical volunteers are to fulfilling the mission statement of the organization, their buy-in will help get other staff to value and support volunteer involvement.

Maintaining communication between staff and volunteers is crucial. Cole says that apart from orientation, many organizations never revisit the roles for staff and volunteers. She suggests holding quarterly or bi-annual check-in sessions for both staff and volunteers to go over roles, responsibilities and job performance. These meetings also provide an opportunity to address concerns about roles and responsibilities before they rise to the level of conflicts.

The sessions will empower staff and volunteers, Cole says, while raising retention rates. Volunteers will be less likely to quit if they have a voice in their role and are recognized for their importance to the overall mission.

Source: Jennifer Gilligan Cole, President, Cole Community Concepts, Nashville, TN. E-mail: colecommunity@comcast.net

Be Proactive in Promoting Internships

Before you promote a paid or volunteer internship, you must clearly define what you are looking for, says Kathryn Berry Carter, director of volunteer services at St. Jude Children's Research Hospital (Memphis, TN).

Carter suggests creating a job description that defines duties, responsibilities, and the skills and knowledge necessary for the position. "Think of things that you've always wanted to do but never had time for, like conducting customer satisfaction surveys, writing volunteer spotlights or articles for your newsletter, communicating with groups of volunteers on Facebook or other social media outlets and more," she says.

With an internship description in hand, you can begin to search for applicants.

Carter says colleges and universities are a great starting point. "In this economy, recruiting for interns is not difficult. Most students want to do something to set themselves apart from their peers and the competition." She suggests contacting career directors and professors at colleges and universities in your area.

Other ways to promote your internship include listservs at area colleges, universities and technical colleges; college work-study programs; professional organizations; career fairs; your organization's website; and your organization's human resources department.

Source: Kathryn Berry Carter, Director of Volunteer Services, St. Jude Children's Research Hospital, Memphis, TN. E-mail: Kathryn.Berry-Carter@Stjude.org

Youth Corps Training Develops Future Volunteers, Leaders

Engage young people in your volunteer corps and they may become volunteers for life.

Beginning a pilot program in 2008, staff with Midland Care (Topeka, KS) — an independent, not-for-profit community-based organization providing options to families with challenging health care needs — worked with 27 children of staff members and friends, ages 10 to 15, to educate them on becoming volunteers on the Midland campus.

Through three days of training in June, July and August, youth corps trainees learned extensive life skills that will be helpful both as Midland volunteers and in other capacities, says Suz McIver, director of volunteers.

"We set the kids up by the end of the summer to become volunteers on our campus," McIver says, adding: "Kids in this world bring a lot of fresh perspective. Our youth corps training not only enlarges our volunteer base, the kids benefit from it both personally and professionally."

McIver offers suggestions for implementing a teen training program:

- ❑ **Design a character-building program.** Focus on leadership skills, trust, effectiveness, communication and other skills that will help trainees become responsible volunteers and community members.
- ❑ **Keep training numbers small and focused.** Condense trainee spaces to a number that allows one-on-one training and individual attention.
- ❑ **Don't overscript training staff.** Ensure that your program allows for hands-on involvement and decision-making by the teen trainees and is flexible to the needs of each individual training group.
- ❑ **Don't underestimate how well teens can do under this type of a program.** Volunteers and staff at Midland Care found that their teen trainees appreciate the flexibility of being self-led.

The youth focused on five significant categories in determining rules and boundaries for the sessions: privacy, participation, conflict resolution, patient treatment and professional conduct. A fee of $25 per participant helped offset costs.

To share the success of this experience, Midland staff are creating a manual guiding other organizations in building a youth program.

Source: Suz McIver, Director of Volunteers, Midland Care, Topeka, KS. E-mail: smciver@midlandcc.org

Goals Drive Youth Training

Staff at Midland Care (Topeka, KS) initiated a youth corps volunteer training program with the following goals in mind:

- To build and provide volunteer assistance at Midland Care.
- To teach compassion and the joy of selfless giving to youth.
- To listen to new ideas and fresh perspectives from youth volunteers.
- To offer an open learning environment in areas of gerontology, grief, loss and end of life.
- To offer youth companionship to Midland clients.
- To grow youth volunteers into adult volunteers.
- To orient, recognize and evaluate youth who participate in the program.
- To introduce youth to health-related careers.

Consider Asking for Letters of Recommendation

Asking teen volunteers and interns for letters of recommendation is one way to make sure they will be committed to the role. Since commitment is so important in volunteering, why not ask all volunteers for letters of recommendation?

Amanda Vallozzi, manager of volunteer services, The George Washington University Hospital (Washington, D.C.), requires new volunteers to turn in three letters of recommendation before they can attend orientation.

Putting the responsibility of obtaining reference letters in the hands of candidates also shows them that becoming a volunteer is a serious commitment.

With an average of 60 new applications every other month, Vallozzi says being able to determine which applicants will take the role seriously and stick with the commitment is crucial. She says she has had issues with volunteers dropping out after just a few weeks, and requiring letters of recommendation helps narrow down the field to persons who definitely want to stick around.

"We don't want to waste our time and resources, and we don't want to waste the volunteer's time, if they're not serious about the position," she says.

Letters can be written by anyone the volunteer has known for at least a year, except for immediate family. Letters typically come from employers, teachers, professors, friends and neighbors. Vallozzi tells volunteers the letters should read as if the volunteer is applying for a job, detailing personality, strengths and commitment. Letters must be typed (handwritten letters may be accepted if a phone number is included), and Vallozzi says they usually contact at least one of the writers for more information about the applicant.

Requiring letters of recommendation hasn't been a deterrent to recruiting volunteers, she emphasizes. In fact, Vallozzi says volunteers who are serious about the position (which is what Vallozzi hoped to identify by requiring the letters) are happy to provide them.

She notes that the hospital is known for high-caliber volunteers who are punctual, adhere to a strict dress code and are serious about their roles.

Source: Amanda Vallozzi, Manager, Volunteer Services, The George Washington University Hospital, Washington, D.C. E-mail: Amanda.vallozzi@gwu-hospital.com

Advice to Keep Youth Volunteers Motivated

High school and college-age students are invaluable to the volunteer workforce at Deaconess Medical Center and Valley Hospital and Medical Center (Spokane, WA).

Each student session, employees welcome a new group of student volunteers to help with healthcare tasks and shadow them on the job. Students are allowed access to emergency rooms and, in a highly supervised way, operating viewing rooms.

Joey Frost, director of volunteer services, offers advice regarding specific elements when working with volunteers ages 14-22:

- ❑ **Applicant interview and evaluation** — When you interview youth volunteers, discuss specifics about their commitment level and schedules to determine if they are already too overcommitted with activities and school to make time for volunteer efforts. Frost notes that some applicants apply only to appease wishes of parents or a college application board.
- ❑ **References** — Just as with any other position, have students apply for volunteer roles. Call on references to learn the student's level of maturity and responsibility before assigning a specific position. At the medical center where Frost supervises volunteers, staff help determine applicants' ability to handle emergency situations.
- ❑ **Flexibility** — Student volunteers need flexibility in their schedules to accommodate course work. By having a flexible scheduling plan, Deaconess and Valley garner a more dedicated volunteer base. During quiet times, information and guest relations desk volunteers are allowed to study while on duty, allowing them necessary study time while fulfilling a useful role.
- ❑ **Variety** — Responsibility and variety help young people stay excited about volunteering. Frost allows students to move into various areas of the healthcare system each semester to give them a varied exposure and keep them engaged.
- ❑ **Boundaries** — Be clear as to the rules of your organization. With cell phone and iPod usage skyrocketing among teens, Frost makes it clear that these devices are not allowed during volunteer shifts.
- ❑ **Policy review** — Provide volunteers and their parents with a copy of the procedure manual for your institution. Have both the volunteer and parents sign a form stating they've carefully read the manual to prevent future misunderstandings.
- ❑ **Program evaluation** — Utilize your current youth volunteers to determine areas of improvement needed in your program. After speaking with high school volunteers who expressed boredom with some volunteer roles, Frost found she could combine two service areas — pharmacy delivery and front desk — to keep volunteers busy and more efficient in their volunteer efforts.

Source: Joey Frost, Director of Volunteer Services, Deaconess Medical Center and Valley Hospital and Medical Center, Spokane, WA. E-mail: FrostJ@Empirehealth.org

Expand Opportunities With Junior Volunteer Program

Engage young volunteers and you may just have a volunteer for life.

Through its junior volunteer program, Antelope Valley Hospital (Lancaster, CA),has more than 200 volunteers age 14 to 18 who assist with reception, in the gift shop, with patient care assistance and more.

Geri Nunez, volunteer coordinator, started the junior volunteer program three years ago. She shares suggestions to create a successful junior volunteer program:

1. **Have an open mind and give young people a chance.** She suggests working with youth who have a grade point average of 2.0 or greater to allow for children from a variety of backgrounds to participate and succeed.
2. **Conduct a thorough orientation outlining expectations for the participants and their parents.** Nunez, for instance, tells students they're expected to make the call, not their parents, if they're sick or late. She also clearly defines that the students are to treat their volunteer role as a job.
3. **Allow the junior volunteers to lead.** At the hospital, junior volunteers organize a variety of fundraisers for the hospital, including an annual bake sale. Nunez allows the volunteers to organize and manage these events, offering guidance as needed. Funds from these events — averaging $3,000 a year — are used to purchase needed equipment for the hospital.
4. **Conduct regular junior volunteer meetings** to offer guidance, share ideas and create a sense of routine for the program.
5. **Create a board for the junior volunteer program.** Organize an election for offices of president, vice president, secretary and treasurer. Teens who volunteered 100 hours or more at the hospital campaign for these offices.

Nunez has developed a strong rapport with her student volunteers and has found that by being approachable and open minded, she has been able to develop a group of exceptional volunteers.

Source: Geri Nunez, Volunteer Coordinator, Antelope Valley Hospital, Lancaster, CA. E-mail: geri.nunez@AVHospital.org

Nurture Junior Volunteers, Create Volunteers for Life

Even the youngest volunteer can make a difference, says Sherry Hodnett, volunteer and bereavement coordinator, Home Hospice of West Texas (Big Spring, TX), who started the Hospice Halos youth volunteer program three years ago.

Hospice Halos are volunteers age 11 to 14 who assist Hodnett once a week in serving hospice clients. They serve food, read to residents, call bingo, give manicures, help with events and bring roses to families of patients who have died.

Hodnett recommends these steps to create your junior volunteer program:

1. **Spread the word** to volunteers that you're starting a new program and would like to involve their children, grandchildren, nieces and nephews.
2. **Host an orientation meeting** to discuss expectations with volunteers and parents. Share a list of expected tasks, so there are no surprises. Have the volunteer and parent sign a letter stating they are expected to volunteer one day a week, plus waivers or confidentiality forms. Be specific on policies for cell phones, iPods, etc. Give parents information to reach children during volunteer shifts.
3. **Provide complete training and/or in-services needed to begin volunteering.** This includes any tests or screenings, such as a tuberculosis test.
4. **Begin activities under supervision.** Provide and require volunteers to wear T-shirts or badges that identify them as volunteers.
5. **Add youth volunteers to your mailing lists,** so they and their parents receive the latest newsletters or correspondence to stay informed on upcoming events and activities.
6. **At the end of the program or at your annual recognition event, reward youth volunteers** with positive feedback, certificates or a field trip to thank them for their participation. Have the volunteers complete a letter of interest to participate in the program in the upcoming year.

Source: Sherry Hodnett, Volunteer and Bereavement Coordinator, Home Hospice of West Texas, Big Spring, TX. E-mail: bshodnett@hotmail.com

Unique Brochure Captures Teens' Attention

When seeking teen volunteers, you need a recruitment tool that grabs their attention and relates to their lives.

The teen volunteer brochure for Hospice of the Valley (Phoenix, AZ) does both.

Kathy Miller, teen program manager, says staff wanted to show teens the similarities they have with hospice patients — many of whom are senior citizens. So they created a brochure that folds out to a large poster. Each fold tells a story as it reveals a picture of an older adult with a statement relating to his/her earlier life: "I am a Cheerleader," "I am a Linebacker," "I am a Tutor," I am a Prom Queen," "I am a Drummer," "I am a Romeo" and "I am a Ballerina."

Miller says the captions connect teens to the fact hospice patients were once teens themselves with the same likes and goals. The poster can be displayed as an eye-catching draw, while the brochures contain information needed for teens to sign on as hospice volunteers.

A local design company helped create the brochures. Hospice staff got friends and family to be the models.

The brochures can be used year round, with timely information, such as training dates, sent as a separate attachment.

Miller says teens have given great reactions to the brochure and the entertaining photos, which, she says, achieves their goal of grabbing teens' attention while communicating with them on their level about the nature of hospice and what it means to be a teen volunteer.

Source: Kathy Miller, Teen Program Manager, Hospice of the Valley, Phoenix, AZ. E-mail: kmiller@hov.org

Content not available in this edition

Content not available in this edition

Content not available in this edition

Content not available in this edition

These photos are from a brochure/poster Hospice of the Valley (Phoenix, AZ) staff use to create common ground between teen volunteers and elderly clients.

Increasing numbers of hospital and health-related websites are devoting more and more Web space to volunteer-related features. Your website can serve as an additional recruitment tool. It can be used to share the impact of volunteer efforts and recognize top-performing volunteers. And you can offer volunteer-only features that allow volunteers to learn, network with one another and become more fully engaged in your hospital's programs and services.

Online Resources Educate Current, Potential Volunteers

With a quick visit to the hospital website, volunteers and potential volunteers at La Rabida Children's Hospital (Chicago, IL) can find answers to frequently asked questions, or FAQs, about the volunteer system.

Clicking the volunteer tab at the hospital's main Web page and scrolling down to the header FAQs, website visitors find a wealth of information about the volunteer process at La Rabida, from age restrictions to volunteer expectations.

"We added FAQs for two reasons," says Judi Blakemore, manager of volunteer services: "Transparency, so that everyone has the same information, and so that applicants are more knowledgeable from the beginning of the process."

Consider adding a similar component to your website and volunteer brochure to educate others on how the volunteer process works at your organization.

Source: Judi Blakemore, Manager of Volunteer Services, La Rabida Children's Hospital, Chicago, IL.
E-mail: jblakemore@larabida.org

Clean, Precise Volunteering Web Page Serves Hospital Well

The website for George Washington University Hospital (Washington, D.C.) offers volunteers a clean and precise volunteering page.

Visitors to the main page of the volunteering section (www.gwhospital.com/Volunteering) find easy step-by-step instructions on becoming volunteers and are just a click away from finding volunteer opportunities at the hospital.

In the past year, Kristin Urbach, director of customer and volunteer service, has recruited 366 volunteers who have provided 16,000 hours of service. Urbach says the volunteering page served as a starting point for many of those volunteers, guiding them through the volunteering process.

Content not available in this edition

Every month, nearly 1,600 Web searchers access the volunteer page at GWU, she says. Here, Urbach tells us more about this high-traffic online volunteer resource:

How does the clean appearance of your volunteering Web page benefit would-be volunteers?

"Due to the information and appearance of our website, in addition to changing the application process to an online one, we have been able to recruit more candidates."

When volunteers call in inquiring about opportunities, are they simply directed to the Volunteer page since the steps are outlined so clearly?

"When volunteers call about opportunities, we respond to their questions and also provide them with the website address. When they call us, we want to be able to provide great customer service by thanking them for their interest, responding to their questions and directing them to the website. When they do not reach a live person, the voicemail provides our website address and recommends they review it for information. As a result, we do not receive many calls, because the website is informative and user-friendly."

Source: Kristin Urbach, Director of Customer and Volunteer Service, George Washington University Hospital, Washington, D.C.
E-mail: Kristin.urbach@gwu-hospital.com

Volunteering Page Offers Accessible Info

Here's a sampling of the volunteering Web page for George Washington University Hospital (Washington, D.C.):

Volunteer Positions include:

Patient Contact & Clerical Duties
Monday – Friday
8:00 a.m. – 5:00 p.m.
Cardiology (until 4:00 p.m. only)
Emergency Department
Nuclear Medicine
Occupational Therapy
Patient Liaison Office
Physical Therapy (In and Out)
Post Anesthesia Care Unit
Radiation Oncology
Speech Pathology
Surgical Reception
Volunteer Services

Nursing Units – Patient Contact & Clerical Duties
Monday – Sunday
8:00 a.m. – 10:00 p.m.
Cardiovascular Center
General Medicine Unit
General Surgery Unit
Intensive Care Unit
Neurosurgery & Orthopedic Unit
Oncology Unit
Psychiatric Unit
The Women's Center

Online Tool Helps Recruit, Track, Coordinate Volunteers

Could the right software program or online tool save time and increase your effectiveness?

One such online tool is Volgistics (www.volgistics.com), offered by the Volgistics company (Grand Rapids, MI).

Carla Hummel, director of volunteer services, Avera Sacred Heart (Yankton, SD),shares how she uses the online system to recruit, track and coordinate volunteers:

> A strong and flexible database such as Volgistics continues to prove useful even as your program expands. Today, you could be asked to provide data to support the impact your programs are making on the services that your organization provides. Databases make this work easier, and in many times, more professional in appearance.

How long have you been working with Volgistics?

"I am just going on a year with Volgistics. It has been quite a step up from the Microsoft Access program we once used. We were finding ourselves continuously bombarded with more lab requirements and were really maxed out of space with the Access program."

Please describe how Volgistics works for your nonprofit.

"With Volgistics we not only have the room to grow but also have much better control over adding requirements, developing levels of patient contact, managing several locations, pulling reports easily that help in decision-making processes, keeping track of pending requirements not completed, having always-accessible contact information and the ability to sort by assignments, locations, type of volunteer, etc."

Share three examples of how Volgistics has helped you as director of volunteer services:

1. "Just today I came from a brainstorming session where we were discussing starting a new volunteer program in a specific area. I was able to go into Volgistics and pull all volunteers from a geographic area, so that we can send a mailing to generate interest."
2. "We had just started on Volgistics and our infection control committee needed information on how many volunteers would be impacted by requiring a vaccination. We were given specific parameters and were able to plug them into a report and come up with the number of volunteers who would need the vaccinations, therefore calculating the costs associated with the effort."
3. "With Volgistics, we have the standard reports for birthdays, labels and lists by assignment for scheduling or attendance. We also have the ability to flag service groups, auxiliary members, employees or specific programs."

Source: Carla Hummel, Director of Volunteer Services, Avera Sacred Heart, Yankton, SD. E-mail: chummel@shhservices.com

Podcasts Tug at Heartstrings of Potential Volunteers

When visitors browse the Memorial Health System of Colorado Springs volunteer website, they're greeted by Janie, a longtime hospital volunteer, in the form of a new tool appealing to the emotions of potential volunteers — podcasts.

Chris Swanson, web communications and marketing strategist, says podcasts go beyond the words that anyone can glance over and instead use a real person to get people to listen, and hopefully, volunteer.

Setting up a podcast is simple and cheap, Swanson says. Apple computer users may already have GarageBand software, while PC users can download the free software Audacity (http://audacity.sourceforge.net/) for everything needed to record and edit a podcast.

Be careful not to overproduce your podcast, Swanson advises. While hospital staff clean up interviews to take out dead air and sneezes, they leave in background noise and other ambience. By doing so, Swanson says, people are more likely to believe the podcast is just another person talking to them rather than a commercial.

Also, Swanson says, persons being interviewed should tell a story. Have them paint a picture — explain why they volunteer and why others should do the same. This results in people putting more of a human element into their discussion, and others connect better with this.

A podcast can be completed in as little as an hour, but expect closer to two or three hours to interview, edit and upload the podcast to your website.

While Memorial Health System staff do not have statistics on how successful the podcasts are, Swanson says word-of-mouth indicates success. Doctors and others are lining up to be interviewed for podcasts to be put on other sections of the hospital website, Swanson says, adding that people want to be able to share it with their friends, family and colleagues.

Also, Swanson says, results of survey groups show people are reacting well to the Janie podcast as well as other podcasts throughout the hospital website.

Source: Chris Swanson, Web Communications and Marketing Strategist, Memorial Health System, Colorado Springs, CO. E-mail: chris.swanson@memorialhealthsystem.com

Showcase Volunteer Opportunities With Online Slide Show

Enticing potential volunteers with an online slide show of opportunities has helped St. Jude Children's Research Hospital (Memphis, TN) recruit volunteers for two years.

"It is a terrific, visual way for volunteers to learn more about our volunteer opportunities," says Kathryn Berry Carter, director of volunteer services. "Our slide show includes pictures of volunteers in action, a brief description of our available volunteer opportunities and requirements for each position."

She recommends the following tips for creating an online slide show:

- Take photos of volunteers in action as often as you can. Each of the 12 opportunities featured on the site rotate among multiple pictures. "The photos provide ... a mental picture of what the volunteer experience will be like," Berry Carter says. "They can visually see and imagine themselves participating as a volunteer."
- Think about your volunteer opportunities from the volunteers' perspective. What might interest them?
- Do not hesitate to include requirements. "Volunteers need to know what they are getting into and the expectations," Berry Carter explains.
- Keep the postings accurate and up-to-date.

St. Jude typically receives 30 volunteer applications each month. Although there is no way to determine a direct link between the slide show and the number of applications, Berry Carter says roughly half are online submissions, thereby indicating a likelihood of having viewed the slide show.

Source: Kathryn Berry Carter, Director of Volunteer Services, St. Jude Children's Research Hospital, Memphis, TN. E-mail: kathryn.berry-carter@stjude.org

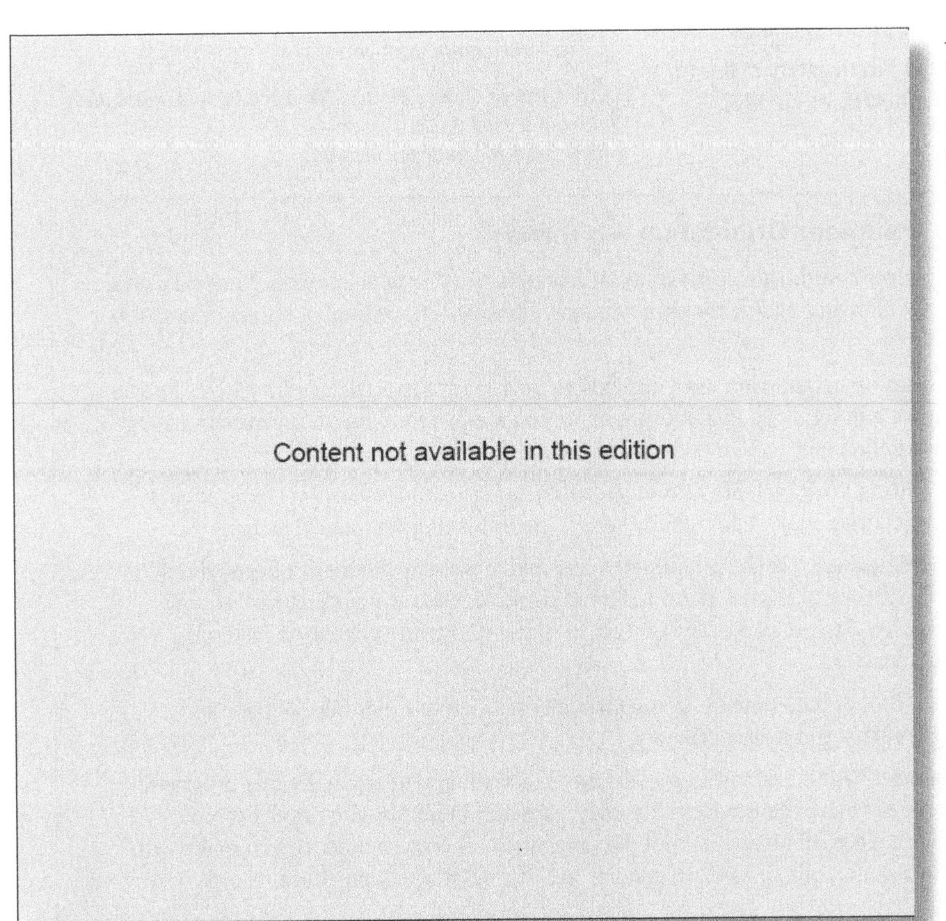

An online slide show for St. Jude Children's Research Hospital (Memphis, TN) features photos and descriptions of volunteering opportunities. (Screenshot photo by Laura Hajaar.)

2012 © Stevenson, Inc.

Medical Center Masters Online Volunteer Orientation

To simplify the orientation process for you and your volunteers, offer it online.

Rather than requiring volunteers to sit through a face-to-face orientation session, an online orientation allows them to work at their own pace in a comfortable setting. Plus, it makes tracking information much easier for your organization.

Making orientation available online makes it accessible to candidates anytime. They can pace their learning and come back for review as often as necessary.

Volunteer coordinators at the University of Arkansas for Medical Sciences Medical Center (UAMS) of Little Rock, AR, began an online volunteer orientation a year ago.

Andrea Stokes, former volunteer coordinator and creator of its online orientation, says that when a volunteer's application is received electronically, he/she is asked to complete the online orientation. To do so, volunteers:

- Read through an online version of the volunteer manual. It covers topics ranging from safety codes to policies and procedures to the history of UAMS.
- Complete four tests and/or forms relating directly to material studied: HIPAA, confidentiality, safety and a volunteer contract.
- Receive an e-mail thanking them for completing the orientation and directing them to contact the volunteer department to schedule an interview.

"Essentially and ideally, all interested volunteers who have scheduled an interview have already completed their online orientation session and have an idea of the way UAMS operates, its history and its mission," Stokes explains.

To ensure a participant actually completes the orientation, she says:

- A database tracks each component of the orientation session.
- Applicants take tests to ensure they have read and understand the material.
- All volunteer applicants must interview with a staff member. During this time, the staff member evaluates the applicant's skill sets.

Source: Andrea Stokes, Clinical Research Promoter, Arkansas Children's Hospital, Little Rock, AR.
E-mail: stokesandreac@uams.edu

Create a Successful Volunteer Orientation — Online

Andrea Stokes, former volunteer coordinator, University of Arkansas for Medical Sciences Medical Center (Little Rock, AR), offers the following advice for organizations interested in starting an online orientation process:

1. **Ignore the belief that online orientation only appeals to people in a specific age bracket.** "People from every generation are willing to try this out as long as you are patient with your instructions and make your module easy to find and easy to understand," she explains.
2. **Be meticulous when editing your website and orientation module.** Stokes says it is important to create a friendly and welcoming look. Additionally, avoid spelling and grammatical errors.
3. **Be prepared to edit and update.** "There is nothing worse than a website that hasn't been edited in more than a year," Stokes says. "If your uniforms have changed, change your pictures. If your confidentiality statement has been revised, don't forget to revise it in your orientation materials. You don't want to mislead volunteers."
4. **Use lots of guinea pigs.** Stokes recommends going through the materials monthly to make sure everything is working properly and is user-friendly.
5. **Invest in a good database.** "Volunteer tracking is essential to maintaining any volunteer program, especially when you are using an online system that may attract individuals who never become volunteers," Stokes says. "Keep all records and, if you can, track all correspondence you make with potential applicants via e-mail, your website, telephone, etc. It's helpful to have those records when you hear from them again."

Newsworthy Links Feature Volunteers in Action

Maximize your news coverage by featuring links on your website. Future volunteers could be captivated by what they see.

At Monroe Carell Jr. Children's Hospital at Vanderbilt (Nashville, TN), links to news sources showing volunteers in action can be found on the center's website at www.vanderbiltchildrens.org. Posting links to news clips featuring engaged volunteers offers a clearly defined window on participating within the organization.

Jerry Jones, director of media relations, explains the best practices of utilizing news sources on a website:

How do you attract media attention at Children's and who originates the idea?

"We use a variety of sources to attract media to Monroe Carell Jr. Children's Hospital at Vanderbilt. Our media team consists of a regional media person, a national media person, a Children's Hospital media person, as well as a PIO (Public Information Officer) in the cancer center and school of nursing. We communicate and work together to pitch stories. Many of the ideas come from us working our beats and talking to the faculty and staff about new research or interesting patient stories."

How does posting the news link to your site work?

"It's important to note that we do not post any video to our sites that a television station airs due to copyright issues. We do post a short summary of the story and links to the story on the media outlet website."

How do you select what to post on the hospital's website? What tips can you share?

"Once a story airs and we think it contains information that is important from an educational point of view or great human interest, we post a summary and link to the story. The same goes for posting print or web articles that someone else has done. It's great to draw attention to these, but be sure not to steal the content. Just link to the original content the media outlet posted. Sometimes these links expire, so you'll want to keep postings fresh and new. We also use the headlines to provide an RSS feed (with the appropriate links) out to our social media networks."

Source: Jerry Jones, Director of Media Relations, Monroe Carell Jr. Children's Hospital at Vanderbilt, Nashville, TN. E-mail: jerry.jones@Vanderbilt.edu

Use Creativity for Monthly Volunteer Features

Key volunteers for Heroes for Children (Richardson, TX) — an organization devoted to assisting families of Texas with children battling cancer — take center stage in the organization's website and blog feature, Volunteer of the Month.

Jenny Scott, executive director and co-founder, offers ways to find and feature special volunteers:

1. Confer with staff to select volunteers who have gone above and beyond the call of duty and should be featured.
2. Seek out volunteer teams (e.g., husband/wife, mother/son or entire family); this allows you to feature more than one volunteer at a time.
3. Select a volunteer who is instrumental at one of your organization's seasonal events, to feature not only the volunteer, but the event as well.
4. Create a questionnaire for the featured volunteer, giving a two-week lead time to return it, with a photo.
5. Ask creative questions. Examples from the Heroes for Children site:
   - *Looking at you, no one would guess that ___.*
   - *What's on your bookshelf? In your iPod or CD changer?*
   - *Who's your hero?*
   - *Where's your favorite place to eat?*
6. Have the director or other key staff person write a paragraph as to why the volunteer is so appreciated.
7. Change it up, so the feature doesn't grow stale. Ask new questions or feature volunteers in fresh ways. Enlist staff to come up with ideas.
8. Follow through with it. Make a concerted effort to update the monthly feature. Don't start a program, unless you're willing to maintain it.
9. Have fun with it! Make sure the volunteer knows he/she is being featured because of his/her contributions. Volunteers don't volunteer for recognition, but they do deserve it.

Source: Jenny Scott, Executive Director and Co-founder, Heroes for Children, Richardson, TX. E-mail: jscott@heroesforchildren.org

Spell Out Volunteer Requirements to Save Time, Funds

Spelling out volunteer requirements from the beginning is an important part of starting volunteers off on the right foot. Officials at the UW Medicine, Harborview Medical Center (Seattle, WA) have taken the time to spell out volunteer requirements on their website, detailing information on health screening, security screening, commitment, age, attendance, sign in and sign out, dress code and background checks.

With 450 to 500 volunteers to manage, Monica Singh, assistant director of volunteer and community services, has found that putting the guidelines front and center is helpful for both the nonprofit and potential volunteers.

"Spelling out the volunteer requirements has been useful in that we have seen an increased rate of accurately completed volunteer applications," says Singh. "The requirements listed are determined by human resources, hospital compliance and privacy policies, process improvement initiatives, state requirements and general experience of working with volunteers."

One advantage of sharing these requirements has been a decrease in the processing time of volunteer applications.

"By clearly stating our requirements up front, volunteer staff spend less time calling volunteer applicants to mail or drop off another required form," she says. "In addition, fewer volunteer applications are mailed back for being incomplete."

This simple step has also had a number of other effects, including:

- Reducing mailing costs.
- Decreasing the number of office phone calls pertaining to specific questions.
- Freeing up volunteer services staff to work on other tasks and programs.
- Reducing misunderstandings and communication errors about basic applicant requirements.
- Speeding up application processing time, allowing volunteers to be interviewed more quickly and efficiently.

Source: Monica Singh, MPA Assistant Director Volunteer & Community Services, UW Medicine, Harborview Medical Center, Seattle, WA. E-mail: ms5@u.washington.edu

How to Create an Effective Volunteer Requirements List

Monica Singh, assistant director of volunteer and community services at UW Medicine Harborview Medical Center (Seattle, WA), shares tips for creating the most effective list of volunteer requirements:

- Hold a brainstorming session with your volunteer services employees. Include key hospital staff who have a vested interest in creating a volunteer program that supports the hospital's HR policies and compliance standards.
- As a team, make a list of all the requirements that a volunteer applicant must meet before they can start volunteering in the organization.
- Get input from all your key stakeholders, so they can provide their perspective and represent the organization's varied interests.

Proceed Slowly With Online Volunteer Descriptions

Adding a college student to your volunteering corps has advantages beyond adding just an extra set of hands.

The Community Service Office at Washington University in St. Louis (St. Louis, MO) has been connecting college students with volunteer-driven community organizations since 1999. One way it does so is through the e-newsletter, The Community Service Connection, e-mailed to thousands of undergraduate and graduate students each week, which features announcements from community organizations looking for volunteers.

Stephanie Kurtzman, director of the university's community service office, says the newsletter is a way for organizations to recruit younger volunteers, which can be especially valuable for groups that work with teens and youth.

"Having a college student talk and work with these young people can make more of a positive impact on these youth than a person at a different stage of life," says Kurtzman. "It's also a way for organizations to find high-quality volunteers, since many of the students have professional skills they are excited to try out in areas such as marketing and graphic design."

The Newborns In Need, Eastern Missouri Chapter (St. Louis, MO) used the e-newsletter to connect with student volunteers. Clem Roeder, chapter president, says the e-newsletter featured an ad seeking students with computer and marketing skills, volunteers to help with organizing donations, plus people to sew, knit and quilt items for the babies.

"We like students as volunteers, mainly because they usually bring an inquisitive mind to the task, so we can spread the word as to the increasing need in our community," Roeder says.

To be featured in the e-newsletter, organizations submit information online or call the department. Kurtzman suggests posting information no more than three weeks in advance of the event. She also notes they do not repeat volunteer submissions, helping keep opportunities fresh.

Sources: Stephanie Kurtzman, Director, Community Service Office, Washington University in St. Louis, St. Louis, MO. E-mail: stephanie.kurtzman@wustl.edu
Clem Roeder, President, Eastern Missouri Chapter of Newborns In Need, St. Louis, MO. E-mail: clemroeder@gmail.com

© 2012 Stevenson, Inc. Published 2012 by Stevenson, Inc.

How often and in what ways do you show your volunteers just how much they are appreciated? Whether you are recognizing individual or group efforts, these ongoing and varied gestures are critical to the long-term success of your program. And those acts of recognition should not be limited to your particular department, but should be a common among all paid employees.

Show Appreciation With Personal Calls to Say, 'Thanks'

Looking for a fresh way to say, "Thanks" to your volunteers?

Whether you do so at your organization's recognition ceremony during National Volunteer Week or simply recognize their efforts for no other reason than just to say, "Thank you," try this idea used by the volunteer department of Seacoast Hospice (Exeter, NH):

Janet Prescott, associate director of community relations and development, says in honor of National Volunteer Week they decided to take a nontraditional approach to show their appreciation.

"Instead of planning yet another event, which most volunteers are too busy to attend, we divided up our list of more than 300 volunteers among 15 of our staff members, including our CEO," Prescott says. "We then asked them to place a simple call to thank the volunteers.

"The volunteers loved getting the thank-you calls, even if the messages were left on their answering machines. For once, we weren't calling to ask them to do something for us. We were simply saying, 'Thank you, we appreciate everything you do!'"

Source: Janet Prescott, Associate Director of Community Relations and Development, Seacoast Hospice, Exeter, NH. E-mail: jprescott@seacoasthospice.org

Support Long-term Volunteers

Here's an idea to celebrate volunteers:

Linda Dean, director of volunteer services, Jackson Hospital (Montgomery, AL), created the Volunteer Emeritus Award to honor five retiring volunteers who served a combined 140 years at the hospital. Through the award, the retiring volunteers and other volunteers of Jackson Hospital serving more than 20 years receive:

- ✓ **An honorary reception:** Complete with refreshments and musical entertainment, the reception features the hospital CEO thanking them for their service and making a plaque presentation.
- ✓ **A special badge:** In exchange for their working volunteer ID badge, retiring volunteers are given a Volunteer Emeritus ID badge that gives access to volunteer areas and events at the hospital.
- ✓ **Lifetime free lunches** with working volunteers and **free parking** in the coveted, gated volunteer parking area.

"The devotion and loyalty of these volunteers is rare in today's world," says Dean. "I felt honored to have these ladies in my program and to witness firsthand the kind of commitment this generation believes in."

Source: Linda Dean, Director of Volunteer Services, Jackson Hospital, Montgomery, AL. E-mail: DeanL@jackson.org

> Recognition events need to remain fresh. Repeating the same format year after year becomes monotonous for long-term volunteers and possibly tedious for organization leadership who participate in the event.

Annual Garden Celebration Features Volunteer Display

Look for ways to jazz up traditional events as a way to thank volunteers for their service and celebrate your organization.

To honor the volunteers who serve at St. Joseph's Health Centre Foundation (Guelph, Ontario, Canada), Volunteer Coordinator Carol McGuigan plans a luncheon.

The outdoor appreciation event relies on good weather and strong attendance of its 50 to 80 volunteers to make for a successful event held in the garden.

The theme Volunteers … Caring, Sharing and Growing, is fitting for the garden celebration, McGuigan says.

As a special tribute, McGuigan creates a display that volunteers see upon their arrival at the event. Located at the entrance of the garden, McGuigan fills the board with photos of volunteers in action throughout the year and adds inspirational quotes that will move the guests.

Follow these guidelines to prepare a display at your next volunteer appreciation event — the volunteers will feel special for the time and effort you put into it:

- Prepare a three-panel, table-top display board approximately 6-x-4 feet, allowing ample room to display your message.
- Use brightly colored graphics, fonts and borders with a garden theme, or a theme that matches your event, to give a cheerful and fun appearance.
- Keep in mind this special group's importance as the display is being prepared, creating a message of appreciation. This luncheon is devoted to your hardworking volunteers for their efforts!

Source: Carol McGuigan, Volunteer Coordinator, St. Joseph's Health Centre Foundation, Guelph, Ontario, Canada. E-mail: cmcguiga@sjhcg.ca

Why Recognize Only One Volunteer Each Month?

Putting a spin on the volunteer-of-the-month tradition, Marcia Todd, coordinator of volunteer services, Alliance Community Hospital (Alliance, OH), recognizes a department of the month.

Featuring an entire department honors many of the 300 volunteers in the 172-bed hospital rather than just one, says Todd. She randomly selects a volunteer department from the hospital's 53 service areas, writes an article about its achievements and submits it to the hospital's internal newspaper, the local newspaper and hospital newsletter, along with information on how to learn more about volunteer opportunities.

The effort helps in recruiting, Todd says. "People can see what each department does, and if it's something they're interested in, we'll get a good volunteer response."

Volunteers being honored receive gift certificates to the hospital gift shop or eatery. Both enterprises are owned by the auxiliary and support the hospital.

Source: Marcia Todd, Coordinator of Volunteer Services, Alliance Community Hospital, Alliance, OH. E-mail: mtodd@achosp.org

Personalization Makes Volunteer Recognition Memorable

Volunteers play a crucial role in the success of many organizations and businesses, and rightly so. After all, you don't want your volunteers' efforts to go unnoticed. But what can you do to make your recognition event a memorable one?

Jona Alborn, psychosocial coordinator, Liberty Hospice Services (Raeford, NC), found a way to express her appreciation that was so memorable, it still has her volunteers talking — a full year after the event.

The memorable recognition took place during National Volunteer Week 2007, when Alborn was volunteer coordinator at Liberty Hospice. To thank her volunteers, she took them out to dinner. Following dinner she presented them with a certificate and award. Sounds pretty run-of-the-mill, right?

Well, this wasn't just any award. Each of her 15 volunteers received a special gift personally chosen for the way it directly correlated to the service he or she provided.

The awards included:

- A tiara for the volunteer with the most hours in 2007. She was crowned Queen of Volunteer Hours.
- A silver sheriff's badge for the volunteer who watched Audie Murphy westerns twice a week with one of the hospice patients.
- A Golden Spoon Award for the aunt-and-niece team who fed patients at a nursing facility.
- Iris bulbs for the gardening volunteer who took plants to the patient he visited.

"We've given them other things throughout the years," Alborn says, "but this is what they are still talking about."

Another plus? The gifts were only $1 to $3 each at a local dollar store. "They were very inexpensive novelty items," Alborn says. But, these gifts are "special treasures to them yet today."

Why were these awards such a hit? Because Alborn specially selected each one for the individual volunteer.

"What they give to us, what they give to the patients is so much energy and life and special experiences," she says. "I was just glad to give something back to them as individuals."

Alborn says the personalization process was not time consuming. In fact, she says, she spent less than two hours browsing the store to find the right items.

The key to such a recognition program, she says, is knowing your donors.

When Alborn was a volunteer coordinator, she says, she tried to develop a relationship with each volunteer. One way she did this was by making an effort to call them to say, "Hi," rather than just when she needed their assistance. Through these friendly conversations, she grew to know the volunteers as more than just names, but as individuals, each with a unique reason for lending his/her time and talents to the worthwhile cause.

So how did Alborn top the 2007 event the next year? For the 2008 National Volunteer Week, she and her staff presented volunteers with T-shirts and entertained them with a magic show.

Source: Jona Alborn, Psychosocial Coordinator, Liberty Hospice Services, Raeford, NC. E-mail: jalborn@libertyhomecare.com

Match Gifts, Personalities

No matter what your cause may be, you can find gifts that say, "Thanks" in a personal way, just by getting to know your volunteers a little bit better.

Whether by phone or personal visit, check in with volunteers as regularly as possible. Along with asking them how their volunteer experience is, ask them a little about what they do outside of your organization, as well.

Then put this knowledge to work to match a gift with the individual.

An avid reader who volunteers for the animal shelter may love a set of books by author/veterinarian James Herriot, while the green thumb who donates hours to your children's program would surely enjoy a pot of whimsical plants such as lambs' ear and bunny-tail grasses.

Honoring the Guild While Setting a Course for the Future

Historically, guilds and auxiliaries have built hospitals and managed their volunteer programs. But as regulatory changes brought paid staff in to manage volunteer programs, guild responsibilities have decreased, along with their numbers.

During the tenure of Mary Kay Hood, director of volunteer services, Hendricks Regional Health (Danville, IN), the average age of guild members was 75 and average age of volunteers was 55. Many volunteers didn't feel the need to join the guild and pay dues when they could do the same duties as volunteers for free.

So guild numbers were dwindling, and the guild was increasingly relying on staff to raise funds and manage the hospital gift shop (key guild duties).

In a strategic planning session for the guild, Hood suggested incorporating the guild into the volunteer services department and doing away with guild dues. After getting administration's support and learning from the hospital attorney that changing incorporation documents would be no problem, she proposed the idea to the guild board, which approved the merger.

Now all volunteers are automatically guild members. Guild members still perform the same volunteering duties, but now they have a fresh group of volunteers to rotate on to their advisory board.

Hood says the trickiest thing about integrating a guild with volunteer services is dealing with guild members who are resistant to change. Two factors in her favor were timing and board leadership.

When she proposed the merger, she says, members were already proposing to retire the guild because of dwindling numbers; current forward-thinking advisory board members realized without a merger, there could be no guild.

"We didn't want to get rid of the guild for historical reasons; they played such an integral role in the formation of the hospital in the 1960s," Hood says. "Now, as long as there are volunteers, there will be a guild. In my mind, this merger has allowed us to 'honor the past and set a course for the future.'"

Source: Mary Kay Hood, Director, Volunteer Services, Hendricks Regional Health, Danville, IN. E-mail: mkhood@hendricks.org

'Powerful' Award Reaps Multiple Benefits

Often, awards and special recognitions can have positive ripple effects.

For instance, at University Hospital at Upstate Medical University (Syracuse, NY), the annual Powerful Partnership Award honors departments that create and value strong bonds with volunteers.

While the award goes to a specific department, its benefits are far-reaching, says Donna Stoner, director of volunteer initiatives.

"The Powerful Partnership Award is a great opportunity for me to put some of the really good aspects of the volunteer program in the laps of the hospital administration, volunteers and staff," says Stoner. "It benefits the volunteers because they learn about what other volunteers are doing and take great pride in the recognition for their department staff.

"Also, I am raising the bar in terms of commitment and focusing on the results of volunteers' efforts."

Each year Stoner invites volunteers to nominate the department they work with for the award based on these criteria:

- **Preparation** — Staff anticipates volunteers' schedules and uses their time and skills wisely;
- **Impact** — Volunteers understand the value of their efforts and their impact on patient care; and
- **Respect** — Staff includes volunteers in meetings, announcements, successes and challenges.

The hospital's Volunteer Initiatives Advisory Council narrows nominees to three. Stoner notifies finalists of their position and issues them special invitations to an annual volunteer appreciation luncheon where the winning department is announced.

Announcing the winner in this setting allows her to shift the focus from the numbers of volunteers and hours served to actual results and accomplishments, Stoner says, noting: "This is a good way to marry the numerical highlights with the quality of work our volunteers do for us."

Source: Donna Stoner, Director of Volunteer Initiatives, Upstate Medical University, Syracuse, NY. E-mail: stonerd@upstate.edu

Honor Volunteers, Those They Serve With Luminary Night

The Visiting Nurse Association of St. Luke's (Bethlehem, PA) has cared for hundreds of hospice patients. To lighten spirits of its current patients and honor those who have passed on, Kathy Lentz, volunteer manager, implemented a luminary event, lighting 170 votive candles along the local hospice house's driveway and meditation gardens.

"The hospice house is a 14-bed facility and each room has French doors which give the patients (and visitors) the opportunity to view the lights," says Lentz.

One afternoon in January 2008, Lentz and eight volunteers set up bags filled with sand and votives, so volunteers, patients and visitors could enjoy them as the sun set.

Lentz estimates the cost at about $1 per luminary. For organizations considering offering a similar gesture, she advises securing donations in advance, organizing a core group of volunteers to manage the process and assigning a project manager. Volunteers are needed to fill bags with sand and votives, to distribute the bags on the grounds, to light the votives and to help clean up when the event is over.

For future luminary events, Lentz plans to gather with volunteers over refreshments once the luminaries are in place as a volunteer appreciation moment.

Source: Kathy Lentz, Volunteer Manager, Visiting Nurse Association of St. Luke's, Bethlehem, PA. E-mail: lentzk@slhn.org

Premiere Movie Event Offers Red-carpet Recognition

Volunteers at the LifeCare Medical Center (Roseau, MN) are treated like stars with a private showing of a newly released movie.

At volunteer movie night, Pam Sando, volunteer coordinator, shows her appreciation for volunteers by treating them to a private screening of a newly released film.

For the annual event, volunteers meet at the local theater and view a pre-selected movie for free. In 2008 nearly 120 junior and senior volunteers watched the exclusive viewing of "High School Musical 3," which carried a G rating, making it appropriate for volunteers of all ages.

"The volunteers loved this event," says Sando. "Some of our volunteers are elderly and don't go to movies often. This was a real treat."

Volunteers enjoyed free popcorn, soda and candy at the private showing, and could bring guests for a discounted rate.

Sando explains why a private movie screening for volunteers is such a hit:

1. The movie screening lets volunteers simply sit and relax for two hours.
2. Movie night requires very little coordination or planning and no setup or purchase of supplies, making a local movie theater the ideal location for a volunteer appreciation event.
3. The evening allowed the theater to reap the benefit of selling tickets to an existing movie for one additional day. The theater offered the medical center a discounted rate for ticket and snack pack pricing, which they purchased on behalf of the volunteers.

Source: Pam Sando and Terry Lamppa, Volunteer Coordinators, LifeCare Medical Center, Roseau, MN. E-mail: Volunteer@lifecaremc.com

Staff Step Up to Serve Up Thank-you Meals to Volunteers

Look for heartfelt ways to say thanks to your valuable volunteers.

At Hospice of St. Tammany (Mandeville, LA), volunteers enjoy a special treat once a year — a meal prepared by staff especially for them.

"This was a great event and very special in the eyes of the volunteers," says Sarah Ferro, office/volunteer coordinator, "because the staff did all the work.

"All of the hospice staff cooked part of the meal," Ferro says. "This year we served brisket, green bean casserole, fresh rolls, fruit salad, fresh spinach salad, garlic whipped potatoes and baked goods."

Having staff prepare the meal adds to the special feeling of the event while keeping costs to a minimum, Ferro notes.

She shares tips on how to create a similar heartfelt event to say thanks to your valuable volunteers:

- ❑ **Plan ahead to get all employees involved.** Have staff sign up to participate at least two months prior to the event. Break the sign-up sheet into four parts: 1) starters, 2) main entrees, 3) paper products and 4) drinks. This allows staff to select what they prefer to bring and gives persons who may not be comfortable preparing food the option to bring plates, forks or napkins.
- ❑ **Send an e-mail to all employees** stating plans for the event. Emphasize the event's importance for volunteer and staff morale. The more excited you are, the more excited your staff will be!
- ❑ **The day of the event, decorate early and have plenty of places available for staff to bring food to keep it warm or cold as needed.** Have extra Crock-pots and ice-filled coolers on hand to preserve the food.

Source: Sarah S. Ferro, Office/Volunteer Coordinator, Hospice of St. Tammany, Mandeville, LA. E-mail: sferro@stph.org

Acknowledge Volunteer Service With Memorial Gifts

Honoring longtime volunteers after they've passed away can reinforce the value of your organization to the late volunteers' families and your current volunteer corps.

At the Mississippi Valley Regional Blood Center (MVRBC) of Davenport, IA, a volunteer who passes away is remembered with a special gift presented to his or her family at the volunteer's memorial service. The gift may be a monetary gift to the person's memorial fund or a plant that acknowledges the volunteer's service.

Kay Parch, manager of volunteer relations at the MVRBC, shares the following steps to take when instituting volunteer memorial gifts:

- Create a budget line item or special fund that allows for acknowledgement of service by longtime volunteers upon their deaths. Parch reviewed internal documents and found volunteers were included in MVRBC's administrative policy up to $50 per memorial.
- Determine whether memorial gifts will be in monetary form to a memorial fund or in the form of a gift to the surviving members of the family.
- Add a personal note to the memorial card acknowledging that specific volunteer and the volunteer's service, such as, "Thank you for sharing your dad with us to serve our organization. The 15 years he served helped many people in need."

Source: Kay Parch, Manager of Volunteer Relations, Mississippi Valley Regional Blood Center, Davenport, IA. E-mail: kparch@mvrbc.com

RSVPs Ensure Seamless Volunteer Recognition Event

Knowing how many volunteers and guests to expect at your volunteer recognition event can allow you to properly plan this important celebration.

A registration form doubled as an RSVP form for the volunteer recognition event for the Arthritis Foundation Eastern Pennsylvania Chapter (Philadelphia, PA), helping organizers know how many attendees and attendees' guests to expect at the March 2010 breakfast buffet/awards ceremony.

Of the nearly 1,300 volunteers invited, more than 210 returned RSVPs.

"We want our recognition events to have a fun and energetic feel to match the personalities of our spectacular volunteers," says Wade Balmer, director of operations and mission integration. "This is an event to pump volunteers up, honor them and show them how much we appreciate their volunteerism. The event isn't long — it's on a Saturday from 10 a.m. to 12 noon. (The Pennsylvania suburb of) King of Prussia is chosen as the location because it's easy to find, accessible via public transportation and several major roads and people can make a day of it and shop at the mall afterwards."

Balmer says that because each volunteer is presented with a certificate of appreciation at the recognition event, asking volunteers to RSVP assisted planners in preparing certificates in advance. RSVPs also afforded event planners the opportunity to gauge attendance and prepare the appropriate amount of food for the group.

Balmer adds that the written RSVP registrations have generated interest from persons beyond the organization's volunteer base, allowing the organization to reach out to these people to offer them opportunities to volunteer and/or give to the cause.

Source: Wade Balmer, Director of Operations and Mission Integration, Arthritis Foundation-Eastern Pennsylvania Chapter, Philadelphia, PA. E-mail: wbalmer@arthritis.org

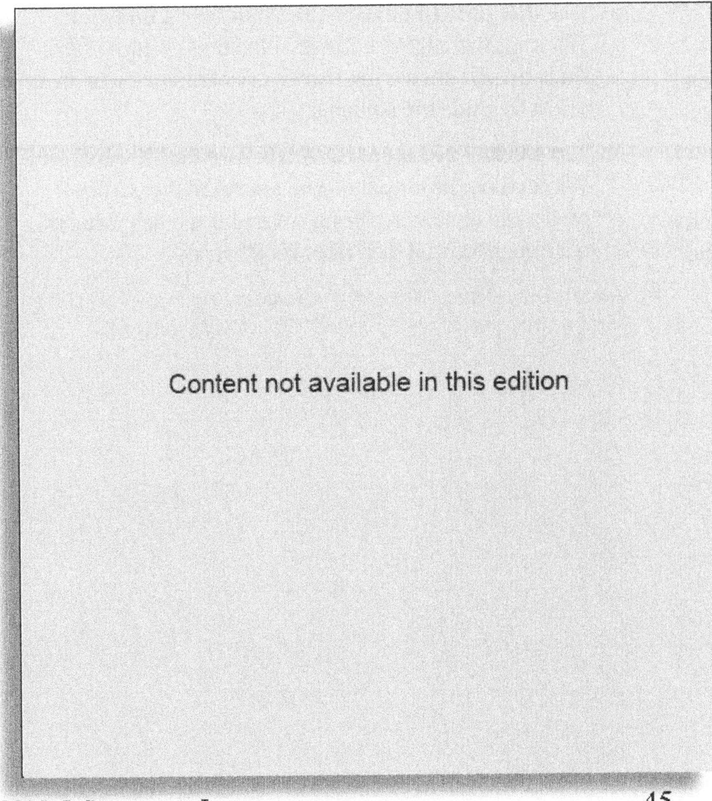
Content not available in this edition

This RSVP form, included in the event flyer and online, helped organizers of a volunteer recognition event for the Arthritis Foundation-Eastern Pennsylvania Chapter (Philadelphia, PA) better plan by informing them who would be attending, and if they would bring guests.

© 2012 Stevenson, Inc. Published 2012 by Stevenson, Inc.

You can only improve your hospital's volunteer programs by continually evaluating what's been done to date. Some of those evaluation efforts are quantitative, while others are qualitative. Make a point to continually seek volunteers' input. Take the time to evaluate their work performance. And even when volunteers choose to end their service with your hospital or health organization, find out more about their decision to leave. What you learn will help to improve your program over time.

Seven Key Steps to Conducting Effective Volunteer Reviews

Seek volunteer input and feedback to improve your program and provide a more rewarding experience for those people who give of their time to your cause.

Joyce White, director of volunteer services, Mayo Clinic (Jacksonville, FL), oversees nearly 500 volunteers. To help keep on top of their needs and to especially make sure that newcomers are having a positive experience, she conducts a formal review when a new volunteer completes three months of service with her organization.

> *Timely reviews of volunteer experience provides valuable information in satisfaction and the continued need for the volunteer program. It also provides notice of potential changes that may need to be made to the program.*

"The three-month review process has made a big improvement in terms of retention and allows that connection where I can be sure that our volunteers share Mayo's values," says White. She notes that Mayo's orientation process covers three months.

She offers suggestions to maximize the results of a review of volunteers following their first three months of service:

1. **Take advantage of a three-month review to insure volunteer's paperwork is in order.** White compares the database to hardcopy files to be sure that all paperwork is complete.
2. **Use the time to get to know the volunteer on a personal level.** White asks pointed questions to determine that the volunteer is satisfied in their current role.
3. **Get a fresh perspective from the new volunteer.** As White's coordinator organizes placement of volunteers, she asks volunteers about their impressions of the interview, placement and interview process. White reviews the process from the volunteer perspective. This step allows White to evaluate the processes and other staff to determine if adjustments are needed. "I believe new people — especially experienced people from the workforce — can offer innovative suggestions and ideas," she says.
4. **Refresh file notes.** White uses the review processes to update note tabs in the volunteer's file to highlight areas of discussion during the review. This keeps the volunteer file current and creates a thorough overview of the volunteer's service time.
5. **Reassure the volunteer.** Encourage the volunteer to come to you to discuss any concerns or problems throughout their service with your organization. The three-month review also familiarizes the volunteer with White and makes them comfortable with coming to her office should they need to see her later for other concerns.
6. **Use this time to answer the volunteer's questions.** Working with many college volunteers, White often finds herself answering career-oriented questions in an effort to guide the students.
7. **Use a tickler system to cover a review for all volunteers.** White recommends creating an organized system that ensures all reviews are being covered in a timely manner once volunteers hit their three-month mark.

Source: Joyce White, Director of Volunteer Services, Mayo Clinic Florida, Jacksonville, FL. E-mail: White Joyce@Mayo.edu

Provide Positive, Structured Evaluations

Jane Merritt, director of volunteer services at William R. Sharpe Jr. Hospital (Weston, WV), offers a standard volunteer evaluation process with a positive twist, noting that managing volunteers with a positive approach aids in retention and overall morale.

"I developed a volunteer evaluation system, as I am a firm believer in evaluations as a positive tool to improve and not a negative to discourage," says Merritt. "Some of the volunteers come in off shifts, and I don't want to lose touch with them or make them feel I do not care. This keeps us in touch."

Here Merritt answers questions about her successful evaluation process:

What is the optimal time for a review of a new volunteer?

"I chose one to two months because it seems enough time to have developed some ideas and understanding, but not too much time to make them feel they are alone and unappreciated."

What are the most common types of problems your evaluation uncovers?

"It has most generally been positive suggestions or questions such as: 'Can I work more time than what I originally requested?' 'Are there other areas that I could volunteer in as well as where I started?' I did have one volunteer request to work in an office setting as opposed to with the patients as they felt uncomfortable. My No. 1 priority is our patients, so I need to know if a volunteer is uncomfortable, because it can be detrimental to the patient."

What kinds of interventions can be taken to remedy issues that arise?

"I am always happy to increase a volunteer's hours if they request it. Also, some areas do not need as many hours at a time, so splitting the volunteer's hours between two departments is a win-win situation. When a volunteer is not comfortable with patients as mentioned above, I reassign them to an office setting. They continue to work many more hours in this setting, filing, typing, answering the phone and allowing the staff more time with patients."

Do volunteers in different kinds of settings or roles need different kinds of evaluations or is one general one sufficient?

"I find that my survey is generic enough to cover all of the different volunteer opportunities at this time. If at some point, it needs updating, it can be done easily. One procedure that I follow to measure and evaluate volunteers is to send a volunteer evaluation as well as an evaluation of the volunteer's service. I send one to the head of the department that the volunteer works under and one to the volunteer to evaluate what they are doing. I usually do this at the end of one to two months of service. This helps me improve the program and takes care of problems before they get out of hand."

Source: Jane Merritt, Director of Volunteer Services, William R. Sharpe Jr. Hospital, Weston, WV. E-mail: Jane.E.Merritt@wv.gov

Boost Newsletter Readership

You put so much effort into your newsletter, but how do you know your readers are actually reading it and understanding it?

Tina Pridgeon, director of auxiliary and volunteer services, Phelps County Regional Medical Center (Rolla, MO), creates the Voice of the Volunteer newsletter each month. She shares four fail-safe ways to ensure newsletter readership:

1. **Add an insert.** By adding an insert about the medical center's quarterly luncheon, Pridgeon has a feel for how many auxiliary members and volunteers read the newsletter based on luncheon attendance.
2. **Include important dates on front.** By listing important upcoming events on page one next to the President's Report column, she ensures volunteers, auxiliary members and medical staff know what is happening each month. The Dates for Your Calendar column includes important meeting information, dates of blood drives, other hospital events and holidays.
3. **Circulate to all interested readers.** Pridgeon not only circulates the Voice of the Volunteer newsletter to doctors and auxiliary members, she also makes certain that volunteers receive a copy. Of 500 newsletters printed, 250 auxiliary and volunteer services members receive a copy, 180 go to physicians and medical staff and the remainder are used for marketing purposes in the volunteer office.
4. **Create a special newsletter issue.** Not only is the newsletter chock full of information about medical center happenings, the first issue of every year is devoted to annual reports of officers and chairpersons to inform readers how the hospital auxiliary is doing financially.

Volunteers and staff look forward to the Voice of the Volunteer announcing the quarterly luncheon's speaker and topic, says Pridgeon. "And the front page Dates for Your Calendar section keeps everyone informed in an easy recurring format that can be snipped and clipped to carry in a planner, purse or kept on the refrigerator."

Source: Tina Pridgeon, Director of Auxiliary and Volunteer Services, Phelps County Regional Medical Center, Rolla, MO. E-mail: tpridgeon@pcrmc.com

Collect Valuable Information With Self-evaluations

Evaluations help nonprofits grow stronger and utilize volunteers more effectively.

Staff with the volunteer department at Upstate Medical University (Syracuse, NY) continually evaluate its program. Recently, they had volunteers complete a self-evaluation (shown at right). The 13-question survey, mailed to all volunteers, addressed four areas:

1. Satisfaction with service
2. Requests for additional training
3. Basic safety information validation
4. Comments and recommendations

"While I place greater emphasis on face-to-face casual conversations or phone calls to gauge a volunteer's satisfaction level or level of understanding, this is the best way to reach all volunteers, especially if you really mean it is mandatory and follow up with personal contact," says Donna Stoner, director of volunteer initiatives.

While The Joint Commission, a nonprofit that accredits and certifies healthcare organizations, requires such a survey for her organization, she says the process would be valuable for any nonprofit that works with volunteers.

"We asked thoughtful questions to elicit candid responses," she says. "The questions were chosen and worded very carefully to draw out quality information."

Stoner reads each survey, and if she sees an area of concern, contacts the volunteer for a personal conversation. Otherwise, she and her staff compile the information and are sharing it with the volunteers through newsletter articles and in-service presentations.

Stoner also asks staff from departments that host volunteers to evaluate the program and the volunteers they work with, both formally and informally.

"We speak informally with our department contacts on a regular basis to gauge the quality of our volunteer service, so we can pick up problems before they blossom," Stoner says.

"However, a formal annual department survey given in person is a good strategy," she says. "When I do one it has two parts: 1) Evaluate the volunteer program as a service, and 2) rate each volunteer individually. The goal is to assess our orientation and in-service practices and determine the effectiveness of each volunteer's service from the department perspective."

Source: Donna Stoner, Director of Volunteer Initiatives, Upstate Medical University, Syracuse, NY. E-mail: stonerd@upstate.edu

Content not available in this edition

Annual Feedback Form Results in More Service Hours

An annual feedback evaluation form for Pikes Peak Hospice & Palliative Care (Colorado Springs, CO) serves as an efficient tool to motivate and retain volunteers.

As a hospice standard of practice to evaluate volunteers annually, Pikes Peak Hospice staff developed the form in 2005 to assess volunteer performance factors such as dependability, availability, judgment, attendance and following procedures.

The form, first sent to volunteers for self-evaluation, is based on a simple rating system of "S" for satisfactory performance or "O" for opportunities for improvement.

Once volunteers complete the self-evaluation, feedback is gathered from staff who work with the volunteers. Items such as volunteer achievements or requirements not fulfilled are also noted on the form.

Cathy Woods, director of volunteer services, then schedules a meeting with the volunteer at an off-site location such as a coffee house to discuss what was written by the volunteer and staff, plus additional thoughts from the volunteer services office.

For areas where there is room for improvement, Woods and the volunteer discuss a plan of action. She says the meetings are also a chance for volunteers to voice concerns and discuss if they should continue in their present assignment.

The feedback method helps volunteers, Woods says. Following a feedback session, she notes, they experience a 10 percent average increase in volunteer hours.

"Our retention rate for volunteers has also risen from an average of 1.8 years of service in 2003 to 3.6 years of service in 2007," she says. She attributes the increase to the feedback as well as having additional coordinators working with volunteers, more emphasis on interviewing and orientation, and improved continuing education classes.

*Source: Cathy Woods, Director of Volunteer Services, Pikes Peak Hospice & Palliative Care, Colorado Springs, CO.
E-mail: cwoods@pikespeakhospice.org*

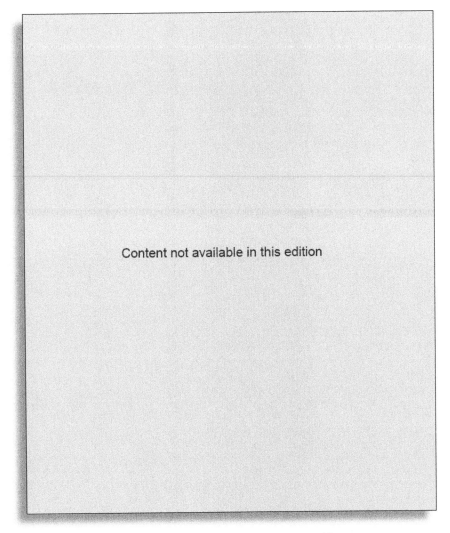

Content not available in this edition

Exit Surveys Pave the Way for Volunteer Program Improvements

Does your volunteer office use an exit interview for volunteers who choose to leave?

Such a tool is proving useful for Jamine Hamner, coordinator, volunteer services, Saint Joseph Health System (Lexington, KY), who based her exit interview form on examples from other hospitals.

"We created this form (shown below) to evaluate our processes," says Hamner. "If a volunteer bows out before they even begin a placement, we want to know if our application/orientation process was too difficult; or if a volunteer withdraws because the assignment wasn't interesting, then what can we do to make this better?"

Hamner says since implementing the form, she has been able to track reasons for volunteers leaving. Some of the reasons included: personal health issues, claims that the staff was unfriendly. or didn't feel they had enough to do, and schedules that didn't allow them to continue volunteering.

To address the scheduling conflict issue raised by the exit interviews, Hamner says they implemented an online system that allows volunteers to access schedules online and schedule themselves for any open shift.

"Of those who had complaints about the staff, we discovered it was two departments specifically that continued to get the complaints," says Hamner. "We continue to work with the department managers to resolve these issues."

Source: Jamine Hamner, Coordinator, Volunteer Services, Saint Joseph Health System, Lexington, KY.
E-mail: hamnerja@sjhlex.org

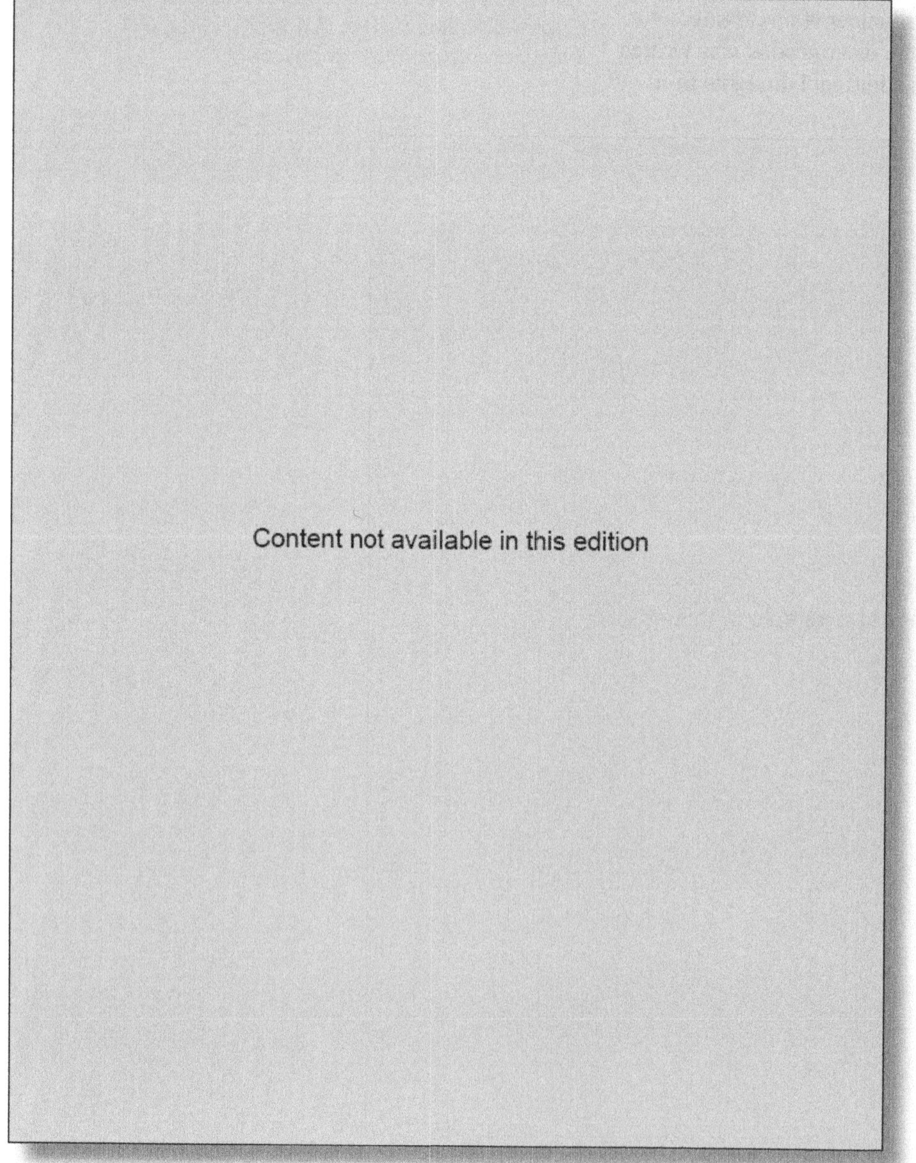

Volunteer Management Essentials for Hospitals & Health-Related Nonprofits.
Edited by Paul Bartush.
© 2012 Stevenson, Inc. Published 2012 by Stevenson, Inc.

Looking for some new strategies and approaches for your volunteer program? Check out this sampling of ideas and examples drawn from other hospitals and health organizations. Use these ideas to start a new effort or as a guide in improving existing programs. Avoid becoming stagnant. Keep testing new approaches at building and strengthening your volunteer program.

Target the Teaching Profession for Skilled Volunteers

Identify profession-specific volunteering options within your organization, then work with members of that profession to identify and recruit persons for those opportunities.

That concept is working well at Children's Medical Center (Dallas, TX), where a simple volunteer inquiry has become a successful teacher volunteer pilot program. Cassie Collins, director of volunteer services, says area teachers began calling on Children's, looking for opportunities to volunteer during their summer and vacation breaks. Because of the strong and consistent interest in volunteering shown by teachers, Collins says, staff developed a volunteer program that specifically targets the volunteer assistance of teachers.

For many individuals, it is very rewarding to offer talents that they are otherwise paid to perform. This can be especially true for individuals who are not currently employed to perform these functions.

Piloting the program in summer 2008, seven teachers became volunteers to assist the center during their summer months and school vacations. Merging the schedules of teachers along with the existing student volunteer training schedule seemed a perfect solution for these two groups of volunteers, Collins says.

During the pilot program, seven teachers served 228 volunteer hours.

"Because we deal with pediatric patients from birth to 18, teachers have the skill set we need to work with our patients," says Collins. "They work well with children and with their parents by showing caring and love. Teachers have the proper training that we need."

Volunteer opportunities closely related to the teaching profession include serving in the classrooms as a tutor, assisting with the art program or family resource center and becoming a sitter. Teacher volunteers can also opt to work in an office environment, if they wish to step away from their typical career setting.

Teachers are offered two summer session options during which they commit up to eight hours per week over five consecutive weeks. Four training options are available to the teacher volunteers based on their areas of interest.

This summer, organizers expect seven to eight new teachers will be on board to serve along with two returning teachers in the specially designed volunteering program.

Source: Cassie Collins, Director of Volunteer Services, Children's Medical Center, Dallas, TX. E-mail: cassiecollins@childrens.com

Take Steps to Establish Volunteer Pilot Program

Interested in beginning a volunteer pilot program within your organization that targets a specific professional group?

Follow these three steps, says Cassie Collins, director of volunteer services, Children's Medical Center (Dallas, TX), which is in its second year of a pilot program that taps teachers as volunteers:

1. Track interest of different professional groups and determine what is attracting this particular profession to your organization.
2. After identifying the group's interest, evaluate your current programs. Do you have something already that is a fit? If not, meet with other department heads in your organization to find the right placement. Offer the group several placement options and keep them informed of their progress.
3. Specify a timeline for piloting the project — three to six months typically works best.

Shape Volunteer Leaders

Volunteers at Children's Mercy Hospitals and Clinics (Kansas City, MO) are taking the lead as members of the hospital's Volunteer Advisory Council (VAC).

"VAC was started about eight years ago to bring volunteer leadership to the forefront of our hospital," says Lynn Hardy, program manager. "We knew that we had a number of strong and capable volunteers who could be instrumental in assisting the volunteer services department and the hospital in numerous ways, if given the opportunity."

The group's purpose or mission, as defined by the council itself, is threefold:

1. Provide advice and consultation for volunteer services,
2. Provide advocacy within the hospital, as well as the community, and
3. Provide fundraising opportunities for the hospital.

Additionally, the 26-member VAC assists with volunteer recognition events and frequently represents the hospital at community events.

VAC members are volunteers who demonstrate extraordinary dedication and concern for the patients, families and staff and are willing to go the extra mile to serve the hospital, Hardy says. VAC is not an auxiliary, the program manager notes. Rather, it represents the "greater hospital volunteer population," all 750 of them.

To become a VAC member, volunteers are nominated by supervisors, invited by volunteer services staff or self-nominated. Membership is limited to three years.

"In a time when it is more and more difficult to find folks to serve on boards, we've found that our volunteers love serving on the VAC," Hardy says. "They truly appreciate the opportunity to serve."

The VAC meets biannually. Three subcommittees meet as needed.

"It is my belief that the VAC has been as successful as it has because the volunteer services department makes a conscious effort to let them be as independent as possible," Hardy says. "They are at their best when they create and implement an idea or project totally independent of volunteer services."

Source: Lynn Hardy, Program Manager, Children's Mercy Hospitals and Clinics, Kansas City, MO. E-mail: lhardy@cmh.edu

Third-party Groups Volunteer to Benefit Hospice

For nearly 20 years, the Hospice Foundation of Western New York (Buffalo, NY) has been working with third-party groups who volunteer their time and resources to organize events and raise money for the nonprofit. The groups, termed "Hospice Helpers," include teams of volunteers from area companies, organizations and community groups.

"Most of our Hospice Helpers hold their events in memory of their loved ones who were cared for by hospice," says Laura Brann, development officer. "To them, their event is important, and it's just as important to us that they enjoy their experience in working with the Hospice Foundation."

In 2010, some 75 companies, organizations and groups became Hospice Helpers, coordinating various activities such as:

- Golf tournaments
- Bake sales
- Auctions
- Concerts
- Dress-down days
- Walks/runs
- Lunches/dinners
- Raffles

When it comes to managing third-party groups, it's important to have guidelines.

"We encourage our Hospice Helpers to be creative; however, we do not allow sales-based activities," says Brann. Also, "We will not approve any Hospice Helpers activities and will not allow them to use our name and/or logo until they have filled out an application and their fundraiser has been approved by our foundation."

Once the event is approved, foundation staff work with each volunteer group to help its event succeed, she says. "Some need our hospice volunteers there to work at their event, some need a staff representative to speak at their event and some need media support such as press releases or media alerts."

Keeping tight communication with these groups is also key. "We are communicating two times per year, even when it's the off season for their particular event," says Brann. "This leads to a high retention rate for our groups."

The Hospice Foundation uses many methods to encourage volunteer groups to take on fundraising projects, including letters and e-mails, phone calls, a Facebook page dedicated to promoting Hospice Helpers and a Web page on the hospice organization's website dedicated to Hospice Helpers.

The Hospice Foundation also lists any group that raises $250 or more in The Center for Hospice & Palliative Care's quarterly newsletter, which has a circulation of 40,000.

Source: Laura Brann, Development Officer, Hospice Foundation of Western New York, Buffalo, NY. E-mail: lbrann@palliativecare.org

Teen Volunteers Meet Strict Criteria to Enter Popular Program

Offer young people rewarding opportunities to give of their time and you may just have a volunteer for life.

Engaging and challenging teens in volunteering opportunities is the goal of the Teen Scene volunteer program at University Hospital Case Medical Center (UHCMC) in Cleveland, OH. Carol Polivchak, manager of volunteer services, says the program utilizes the efforts of 100 teen volunteers each summer (mid-June through mid-August).

The program is not only a benefit to the patients and staff of UHCMC, Polivchak says, it gives teens hands-on experience in a multitude of volunteer roles.

"It's inspiring to see the transformation that takes place during a short period of time," says Polivchak, who begins accepting applications for the highly successful summer program each January. "Many teens begin the program reserved and lacking confidence; by the end of the program, they have gained confidence and are much more articulate."

Because the Teen Scene volunteer program has gained such prominence over its six-year run, the hospital receives far more applications than there are spaces available.

With acceptance to the volunteer program so competitive, the volunteer services manager says, UHCMC has developed a strict series of guidelines to help select the top candidates. Those guidelines are:

1. The candidate must complete essay questions relative to the position by submitting a typed response with application materials.
2. A guidance counselor must submit an evaluation of the student volunteer.
3. During the interview process, students receive a tour of their areas of interest to ensure they are up for the challenge of that position. Placing applicants in the environment will allow them to confirm whether that is the best placement for them.
4. Remain strict on policies. UHCMC allows only one week off for student volunteers. Those volunteers requiring two weeks off during the program are not accepted.
5. Gain parental commitment to student volunteer schedules and to transporting volunteers who cannot drive themselves.
6. Be firm on deadlines. Accept no applications after the posted registration date.
7. Be compassionate to those who are not accepted and encourage them to apply the following year.

Source: Carol Polivchak, Manager of Volunteer Services, University Hospital Case Medical Center, Cleveland, OH. E-mail: carol.polivchak@uhhospitals.org

Bring-a-friend Option Attracts Volunteers

Get double the mileage from your next volunteer recognition event by turning it into a volunteer recruitment opportunity as well.

At Covenant HealthCare (Saginaw, MI), volunteers attend a Bring a Friend event with a friend who is a likely volunteer candidate. The event serves to both show appreciation to current volunteers as well as recruit new ones. Attendees enjoy hors d'oeuvres and cocktails as they mingle with staff in a casual atmosphere, says Sarah Knochel, volunteer manager.

"Volunteers can be the best recruiters and ambassadors for an organization," says Knochel. "If they enjoy what they do, then they will want friends and family to have the same benefits from volunteering at the organization."

For organizations considering hosting a double-duty event to both recognize existing volunteers and recruit new ones, Knochel offers this advice:

- ❑ Spread the word to all volunteers, encouraging them to bring a guest who is a likely candidate for volunteering. Be sure that volunteers understand that their spouses (who may not currently be volunteering) are welcome and encouraged to attend.
- ❑ Prepare an educational display showing photos or video of volunteers at work throughout your organization. Include information on the types of volunteer roles available as well as a description of your volunteer services department.
- ❑ Have plenty of extra volunteer applications available.
- ❑ Spotlight volunteer needs and related duties along with offering a volunteer fact sheet.
- ❑ Present a program that highlights benefits of volunteering at your organization and shares areas of need.
- ❑ Have staff members who can answer questions attend.
- ❑ Couple the event with volunteer recognition to show potential volunteers the value you place on volunteers.

Source: Sarah Knochel, Volunteer Services Manager, Covenant HealthCare, Saginaw, MI. E-mail: sknochel@chs-mi.com

Labels Draw Awareness to Volunteer Efforts

Consider labeling your volunteer-assembled items and volunteer-created projects to draw attention to their efforts within your organization.

Volunteers at LifeCare Medical Center (Roseau, MN) fulfill a great array of volunteer tasks. Whether assembling information folders, admission packets and pamphlets or filling plastic eggs for the annual Easter egg hunt, they place a sticker on the item that reads, "Assembled by the caring hands of our Volunteers at LifeCare Medical Center."

"These labels trigger the minds of those utilizing the information that a volunteer's hands created that item," says Pam Sando, volunteer coordinator, "drawing awareness to our volunteer efforts and also putting our name on each item."

Assembled by the caring hands of our Volunteers at LifeCare Medical Center

Source: Pam Sando and Terry Lamppa, Volunteer Coordinators, LifeCare Medical Center, Roseau, MN.
E-mail: Volunteer@lifecaremc.com

Volunteer Guilds Provide Lifeblood to Children's Hospital

Do all you can to encourage members of guilds or other subgroups that support your cause.

Seattle Children's Hospital (Seattle, WA) boasts an impressive 500 guilds with a total membership of 7,000 — the largest guild association network for any hospital in the United States. Each guild represents a group of members who band together with the mission to assist the hospital by supporting its uncompensated care and research programs.

When a guild forms — typically a group of like-minded individuals who feel strongly about the work done at Seattle Children's, a 250-bed facility ranked eighth in the United States by U.S. News and World Report that specializes in cancer and craniofacial treatment — representatives of that new guild contact Aileen Kelly, executive director of the Seattle Children's Hospital Guild Association.

Guild association staff then send a profile questionnaire to the new guild's leaders, who return the completed form, along with $25 in dues per member.

The profile questionnaire lists the founding members and provides details about the guild including the guild's name and the inspiration behind forming the guild. The guild's leaders attend an orientation that takes them through the association's guidelines, policies and fundraising tools.

Kelly offers the following advice when instituting guilds at your nonprofit:

- ✓ **Make it easy and fun.** Simplify the process of registering as a guild for your nonprofit. Welcome each guild's uniqueness and creativity.
- ✓ **Provide high-touch opportunities.** Ask members of each guild to conduct meetings at your location and offer to have organization leaders speak at guild meetings.
- ✓ **Take every opportunity to show your appreciation.** Remind each guild often of the importance of their mission and impact of their generosity.

Source: Aileen Kelly, Executive Director, Seattle Children's Hospital Guild Association, Seattle, WA.
E-mail: Aileen.Kelly@seattlechildrens.org

Guilds Represent Many Walks of Life

More than 500 guilds representing 7,000-plus members share one passion: raising funds for Seattle Children's Hospital (Seattle, WA).

Nearly 60 of the hospital's 500 guilds gross $25,000 or more each year, with some reaching upward of $1 million a year to benefit the hospital, says Aileen Kelly, executive director, Seattle Children's Hospital Guild Association.

Many of the guilds consist of people with a common interest. For some, that interest is related to the hospital. For others, it's not.

For example, a group of motorcycle enthusiasts named the Imagine Guild hosts a motorcycle ride where the destination includes a barbecue and live entertainment and is preceded by a bikers' gala and auction.

Another group, Pink Polka Dots, includes 12- to 13-year-olds who lost a friend to a brain tumor. This guild raises nearly $40,000 a year for brain tumor research selling homemade greeting cards and hosting an annual golf tourney.

Dreaming Day Retreat Brings Amazing Results

Don't be afraid to dream big.

At the Make-A-Wish Foundation of Utah (Murray, UT), CEO Chriss Sharer had an interesting concept to motivate board members to raise funds: a retreat that had nothing whatsoever to do with money or fundraising. Instead, the board spent the day imagining the difference that a planned capital campaign could make for the families the foundation served.

If successful, the capital campaign would fund the Wishing Place, a magical setting where children with life-threatening medical conditions can start the process of making their wishes come true.

Important pre-retreat groundwork and the right approach at the event combined to light a fire under the board members that helped raise a record $2.6 million toward the Wishing Place.

Prior to that retreat, foundation staff polled 400 families of "wish" children, says Sharer. "We asked how we could make wishes better. We got some interesting and surprising responses, which eventually caused us to rethink completely the way we delivered our services in our new facility."

They shared results at the retreat, focusing on dreams the capital campaign could turn into realities for children and families the organization serves. By retreat end, Sharer says, "We had described some stunning differences. Everyone really wanted to take the next steps because it would so transform our services."

They followed the first retreat with a second to explain what would be expected of the board if the project moved ahead, and a third retreat on major gifts fundraising that ended with pledges from board members.

"This was transformational fundraising for us," says Sharer. "Prior to that campaign, the largest gift we had ever received was one $40K grant to build an online presence. In the campaign, we got three $500K gifts and four $100K gifts."

Another benefit of the Dreaming Day retreat? It helped everyone understand the difference that could be made through their efforts, says Sharer, who adds, "That is really why anyone gives money to anything — to make a difference."

Source: Chriss Sharer, CEO, Make-A-Wish Foundation of Utah, Murray, UT. E-mail: csharer@makeawishutah.org

Outdoors-oriented Organization Reels in Volunteers

Reeling & Healing Midwest — a nonprofit based in Branch, MI, and Chicago, IL, that offers fly-fishing wellness retreats for women with cancer — is run solely by volunteers.

More than 300 volunteers help to serve the nonprofit's mission to provide participants with a one-of-a-kind experience, on and off the river, which renews their spirit and hope through the elements of fly-fishing, nature, peer coaching, positive camaraderie and support.

Volunteer roles run the gamut from updating the database to following up with participants after a retreat to assisting at information booths to teaching fly-fishing.

Retreats are one to two-and-a-half days in length. Land volunteers work approximately eight hours for a one-day retreat and 30 hours for longer events. River helpers, guides and instructors can also work anywhere from six to 30 hours depending on the length of the retreat.

Opportunities are plentiful for volunteers who would like to assist in the river, as a retreat of 14 participants requires three land volunteers and 16 to 18 river volunteers.

To find volunteers who are savvy outdoorsmen and women, look in these places:

- Check with your local Department of Natural Resources to find educated and trained professionals willing to volunteer with your outdoor organization.
- Host a booth at fishing or boating expos to interest outdoor enthusiasts and lure extra volunteers.
- Offer a free fly-fishing seminar and ask audience members to consider volunteering.
- Use the tried-and-true method of word-of-mouth recruiting; it's been critical to the Reeling & Healing Midwest organization.

Source: Cathy Sero, President, Reeling & Healing Midwest, Chicago, IL. E-mail: csero@reelingandhealing.org

Extra Volunteer Commitment Keeps Event Fresh

When recruiting volunteers to help with your special event, consider asking them to commit to a full year of planning as well.

Nicole DeCelle, associate director, signature events, Albany Medical Center Foundation (Albany, NY) ,says, "During the 'off-season' (September–February), our volunteer committee meets every other month to explore new ideas and initiatives to keep our event fresh and exciting, and to begin planning event details and strategies."

This is especially important, says DeCelle, because one of the foundation's biggest challenges in organizing the Light Up the Night event is to maintain its uniqueness against a backdrop of so many other charity events and benefits.

"We constantly have to be aware of the timing for the event and coming up with new creative ways to make our event stand out from those of other organizations. One strategy to overcome these challenges is to benchmark against what other successful organizations are doing, and what our committee members have seen and heard about other events in the area."

Source: Nicole Stack DeCelle, Associate Director, Signature Events, Albany Medical Center Foundation, Albany, NY. E-mail: StackN@mail.amc.edu

Partner With Other Nonprofits to Sell Volunteerism at Job Fairs

Look for fresh, creative ways to reach people with your message of volunteering.

At Blessing Hospital (Quincy, IL), the ongoing need for qualified volunteers led Susan Dean, director of volunteer services, to host a booth at a local job fair. She did so along with several other area nonprofits including the Red Cross, RSVP and other organizations from the Center for Effective Nonprofits.

With a booth near the fair exit, organizers attracted passersby with an offer of a free calculator printed with the words Volunteers Count if they participated in a quiz.

The 13-question quiz determined life expectancy based on habits. Participants not only learned anticipated life expectancy, but that simple changes — doing a daily problem-solving game, exercising regularly and eating properly — can add years to their lives.

Most importantly, they learned that volunteering adds two years to life expectancy.

With this revelation, Dean says, participants scooped up brochures about volunteerism in the Quincy area. Almost 400 people entered the job fair with 20 percent of those stopping by the volunteer booth.

As the attendees were there to attend a job fair, Dean and others emphasized how volunteering is a useful way to gain new work skills while searching for employment.

Here are suggestions to capture volunteers with your booth:

1. **Order your giveaway in advance.** Dean ordered the calculators in advance and put her organization's contact information on the calculator boxes. While she had expected about 25 attendees to stop at her booth, when that number tripled, she says she was glad she had extra calculators and quizzes on hand. Cost of the calculators was $3 each in lots of 100.

2. **Share ideas with other volunteer organizations.** Coordinating with other nonprofit groups allows more people to share in responsibilities and benefits.

3. **Arrive early.** Dean says attendees were waiting to enter one hour prior to start time.

4. **Create a PowerPoint presentation that shows volunteers enjoying their efforts.** A PowerPoint presentation or slide show of volunteers in action brings volunteering to life and shows fair goers that volunteering can be a fun experience.

5. **Emphasize reasons to volunteer.** In the booth's display, emphasize that volunteers gain work and life experience, self-confidence, improve health, increase life expectancy, experience diversity and find networking opportunities. Also, note that in some cases, volunteering leads to paid job positions!

Source: Susan Dean, Director of Volunteer Services, Quincy, IL. Phone (217) 223-8400. E-mail: sdean@blessinghospital.com

Volunteer-run Street Fair Is Big Fundraiser for Hospital

Knowing your unwanted items can help someone else is a great feeling. That's one reason why the annual Street Fair for the Hospital Aid Association (Wolfeboro, NH) is such a big success.

Another reason? Volunteers have taken the event and run with it, turning it into a must-attend event that draws thousands of people and keeps volunteers busy for months, planning, sorting and pricing merchandise.

The street fair resembles a giant flea market, offering up for sale everything from plants to boats.

Jane Wass, co-chair, says they set up the two-day August event on the grounds of Brewster Academy, an independent secondary school for boarding and day students. Items are separated by category under multiple tents and sold directly to the public.

Grouped into like categories, items include books, plants, sporting goods, jewelry, toys, dishes, appliances, electronics, clothing, white elephant items and food.

Big-ticket items, like boats, cars and antiques, are sold by auction.

All proceeds from the event go to Huggins Hospital (Wolfeboro, NH) to buy equipment for patient care. This past year, the Hospital Aid Street Fair presented Huggins Hospital with a check for $100,000.

The Hospital Aid Association is supported and run by volunteers. The street fair, started in 1937 by Ethel Black using a volunteer's garage, has grown — along with the association — over the last seven decades.

Now, items are collected and stored in three 5,400-square-foot barns. Sorting, marking and packing of items is done by 50 to 60 volunteers, while 500 volunteers lend a hand throughout the two-day event.

Wass and her husband, Bob, have co-chaired the event for six years along with volunteer Mary O'Neill, who handles the business end.

Besides using the donations to raise money for the hospital, the organization frequently donates items to other nonprofit organizations in the community. Medical supplies or equipment, like wheelchairs or crutches, are given freely to the public. They also donate to the homeless and anyone else in need.

Source: Jane Wass, Co-Chair, Hospital Aid Association Inc., Wolfeboro, NH. E-mail: winterharbor@yahoo.com

Work With, Praise and Thank Your Run/Walk Volunteer Crew

Volunteers are crucial to the ongoing success of the Children's Red Balloon Run & Relay, the signature grassroots event for Children's Medical Center (Dallas, TX).

Participants in the annual 5K run/walk are encouraged to raise $100 each for the hospital and can designate their funds to one of the 106 specialties it offers, says Preston Walhood, campaign director for Passion for Children's (Dallas, TX), a nonprofit designated for creating and supporting fundraising efforts for Children's Medical Center. He notes that the October 2010 event drew 3,476 participants, 2,179 of whom raised funds for the hospital.

The weekend event requires 30 volunteers for Friday set-up, 50 for Saturday set-up, 75 or more to help during the run, and 60 to help with post-race cleanup. During the event, volunteers coordinate fundraising efforts, help with event signage, staff rest stops along the race course and act as cheerleaders to runners and walkers.

Walhood offers his top four tips for managing volunteers at a 5K event:

- **Delegate.** No event director can work directly with every volunteer. Find a rock-star volunteer who can manage your volunteers for each area. A volunteer coordinator can manage each area of your volunteer pool the day of the event for maximum efficiency.
- **Praise with thank yous and at-a-boys!** Cheer on your volunteers. Offer praise and thanks, and watch the morale of a volunteer group skyrocket.
- **Always be willing to do what you ask them to do.** Every event has trash and, therefore, needs a trash crew. Make sure that you grab a pair of gloves and hop in with your volunteers and participate in what they are doing. Always make them feel like they're working with you, not for you.
- **Be gracious and thankful, knowing that volunteers don't have to be there.** If they want to be in charge of an area, let them be and thank them for being in charge! If they feel appreciated and needed, you have succeeded.

Source: Preston Walhood, Campaign Director, Passion for Children's, Dallas, TX.
E-mail: preston@passionforchildrens.org

Ring in Holiday Spirit With Ornaments That Promote Your Cause

It's never to early to begin planning your holiday fundraiser, especially if it involves ordering special merchandise such as holiday ornaments.

At Gaston Hospice and Grief Counseling Services (Gastonia, NC) in 2008, a group of five volunteers ages 70 to 80 affectionately known as the Wild Women successfully managed the first-ever sale of ornaments to benefit the organization, says Jennifer Jones, volunteer coordinator. The premiere event featured snowflake, bell and ball ornaments handcrafted by local North Carolina potters.

"The Wild Women spent 150 hours of volunteer time preparing the ornaments for the sale," says Jones. "They packaged them and made them look beautiful. We couldn't have done it without them!"

Gaston Hospice offers the following tips for making an ornament sale a success:

1. Be careful not to order too many ornaments the first year to avoid cutting into profits. If you do have a surplus, offer extra ornaments at next year's sale. Many people enjoy collecting a series of ornaments and are willing to pay for past years' items to complete their collection.
2. Start small and let the fundraiser grow year after year.
3. Ask area restaurants, gift shops and other retailers to display ornaments and distribute order forms to increase exposure of the ornament sale.
4. Publicize the event. Ask your local newspaper to run an article about your ornament sale and make sure you mention it in your newsletter as well. Also, send out postcards and order forms to the people on your mailing list.

Source: Jennifer Jones, Volunteer Coordinator, Gaston Hospice and Grief Counseling Services, Gastonia, NC. E-mail: cunningj@gmh.org

Websites Offer Ornaments

If you are fortunate enough to have volunteers who are creative and crafty, now is the perfect time to ask them to make unique ornaments to promote your cause this upcoming holiday season. Whether they use wood, beads, fabrics, stained glass or another medium, an ornament handmade by your volunteers is sure to be prized by your staff, clients and supporters.

Would you rather seek out a company to mass produce an ornament that captures the spirit of your cause? Here are some websites that offer such products to get you started:

Tom Pollard Designs — www.tompollarddesigns.com/

Calliope Designs — www.calliopedesigns.com/

Russell Rhodes — www.russellrhodes.com/

Content not available in this edition

This full-color postcard helped kick off the first-ever holiday ornament sale for Gaston Hospice (Gastonia, NC).

Music Soothes Patients, Staff

Here's an example of how volunteers' hidden talents are now cheering staff, patients and others at High Point Regional Health System (High Point, NC):

Since 2004, the volunteer department has provided a soothing atmosphere in the hospital lobby by having volunteers play the piano.

Annie Riddick, director of volunteer services, says the development department provided a grand piano and she recruited volunteers to play it. She says it's been a really great service since many people coming into the hospital may be anxious about why they're there, and the music provides comfort.

The position of volunteer pianist requires almost no recruiting, Riddick says. After hearing the piano music, many volunteers step forward and ask to play, and other listeners recruit friends and family they know who play.

The volunteers play one to three hours once or twice a week, says Riddick, adding that patients often come down and listen while in the hospital.

Source: Annie Riddick, Director of Volunteer Services, High Point Regional Health System, High Point, NC. Phone (336) 878-6000. E-mail: ariddick@hprhs.com

Volunteers Work at Getting a Laugh for Wellness

At Lankenau Hospital (Wynnewood, PA) patients not only receive top-notch care, they also can expect a laugh or two during their stay.

That's because at the hospital, a group of dedicated volunteers are members of a caring clown organization that is a living example of laughter as the best medicine. Through the hospital's Humor Prescription Program, volunteers — dressed in clown garb — provide gentle humor that lessens the anxiety often felt by patients and their families and helps take their minds off their health issues.

These volunteers do much more than don face paint and brightly colored clothing in order to fulfill their important tasks. They attend an intensive six-week training program where they learn the art of assisting patients through the use of gentle humor.

The Bumper "T" Caring Clowns, Inc. (Barrington, NJ) is a volunteer organization dedicated to making a positive difference in the lives of hospitalized patients, their families, friends and caregivers through therapeutic clowning.

The caring clown training, available to interested hospitals, healthcare facilities and related organizations, was developed by professional clown Bumper T. Clown with the assistance of Esther Gushner and Aviva Gorstein. Gorstein worked as a director of volunteer services in a large medical center for 12 years, where she says she saw the value of how light-hearted, gentle humor within the hospital environment could assist patients in their recovery, as well as boost the spirits of patient families, volunteers and staff.

The program requires 24 hours of training involving intensive classroom study and shadowing of an experienced hospital clown before graduation. The clowns dress as doctors in lab coats and scrubs with soft clown makeup and all have doctor names such as: DR Bumper T Clown, funnyboneologist, DR. HuggaBubbe, hug specialist, and DR. Bea Well.

When searching for volunteers to act as caring clowns at Lankenau Hospital, Gorstein looks for the following qualities:

- Older, mature volunteers with life experience. Sensitivity and listening skills are important qualities, so the volunteer clowns can readily recognize body language cues and assess the differing needs of patients at the time of the visit.
- Volunteers who are flexible and not easily thrown by the quickly changing situations that often take place in the hospital environment.
- Fun-loving volunteers who can readily find humor in almost any situation.

Source: Aviva Gorstein, Bumper "T" Caring Clowns and Lankenau Hospital Volunteer Services, Wynnewood, PA. Websites: www.mainlinehealth.org (Lankenau Hospital) and www.bumpertcaringclowns.org (Bumper "T" Caring Clowns, Inc.)

Float Creates Opportunity for Short-term Volunteers

Have volunteers organize a parade entry to build camaraderie and spread your message.

Camitha Whipple, house manager, Ronald McDonald House of Long Branch (Long Branch, NJ), says the nonprofit's float in the annual Columbus Day Parade raises awareness, results in donations and volunteer inquiries and benefits the families they serve. Those families work with the volunteers to create the float and then ride on it in the parade.

Such a project is also a great way to engage groups who want to volunteer on a short-term basis, says Whipple. She offers tips to maximize exposure with minimum investment:

- **Be flexible with your volunteer force.** Every year a group of volunteers solicits for materials, recruits float builders and builds the float, though not always the same group of volunteers. Allowing different groups to participate makes it easier to fill roles and creates variety in the final product.
- **Work with what you have.** Whipple's volunteers look to the season to create an appealing float at low cost. For Columbus Day they use hay bales, scarecrows and corn stalks around a miniature house to create The House That Love Built…in Autumn.
- **Don't be afraid to ask.** Whipple says the parade's organizers donate space to work on the float, plus use of a truck, flatbed and driver. Donating their time to the event benefits them as well, as it allows them to show off their philanthropic nature and share some of the resources that are available in the community.

*Source: Camitha S. Whipple, House Manager, Ronald McDonald House of Long Branch, Long Branch, NJ.
E-mail: camitha@rmh-cnj.org*

Volunteer-assisted Story Project Strengthens Organization

Staff and volunteers at Seattle Children's Hospital (Seattle, WA) gathered 700 moving stories from patients through its Children's Story Project.

Through the program that began in 2006, hundreds of people from the hospital's service region have shared personal experiences, memories and reflections about their experiences at the hospital, creating a historical archive that honors more than a century of providing hope, care and cures for children and families throughout the Northwest.

Mirtha Vaca-Wilkens, media project manager at the hospital, shares details about the project and how volunteers were instrumental in its process:

How long did the project take to complete?

"The project was initiated as part of the public phase of the Campaign for Children's Hospital and was presented as another way for people to give back to the hospital. It officially launched in February 2006 as part of the public launch of the campaign for Children's and culminated September 2008. The Story Project is still collecting stories to this day ... so the project has completed its initial function as a tool to engage the community in our campaign, but it's taken on a life of its own now. People are still submitting stories every day."

What roles did volunteers play in this project?

"In order to have great, robust content when we launched the site, we had to pre-populate the site with stories we collected. As part of this process, we had to sift through tons of personal thank-you letters written to the hospital, calls that had been recorded and transcribed and had to follow up with actual interviews with people we wanted to include in the website. We worked with two volunteers who helped us track down the best stories and who helped us interview people and transcribe their stories to the website. They also followed up with many of these people and kept them engaged in the campaign. Moreover, we had a phone number for those who weren't comfortable submitting their story online. A volunteer would listen to these stories over the phone, transcribe them and post them to the website. Finally, we had a variety of events tied to the campaign where we would make a public appearance with our tape recorder in hand. At many of these events, we were able to interview people and share their story on the website."

How did you go about gaining volunteer help for this project?

"We have a great team of volunteers. All I did was ask Denise Green, our volunteer director, to provide a few people she thought would be interested in helping us with this project. In no time, I had the volunteer help I needed."

Volunteers helped track down the best stories, helped interview people and helped transcribe their stories to the website.

How many volunteers helped with this project? How many hours did volunteers contribute to the project?

"Two volunteers helped and they worked for about six months during the peak phase of the project (when we were collecting the most stories to pre-populate the website). I'd say they probably averaged about 15 to 20 hours per month during that six-month period."

How has this project strengthened your organization and the vital role that volunteers play at Seattle Children's Hospital?

"The Story Project has engaged our internal community in ways we never imagined. It really has brought home the concept that everyone has a story to share. It has also kept us mission-focused and helped to strengthen the resolve that many of us have in ensuring we provide the best pediatric care for our families. Hearing the amazing challenges many of our families face and also the incredible accomplishments their kiddos are able to make despite their diagnoses is both a humbling and character-building experience. It definitely is a reminder of why we come into work every day. The volunteers embody this way of thinking just by the very nature of their role with the hospital. ... This project just helped illustrate their passion for this organization even further."

Source: Mirtha Vaca-Wilkens, Media Project Manager, Seattle Children's Hospital, Seattle, WA.
E-mail: mirtha.vaca-wilkens@seattlechildrens.org

Lightning Source UK Ltd.
Milton Keynes UK
UKOW06f2120020913

216389UK00008B/171/P